Beautiful Savage: An Entrepreneur's Guide to Enjoyment, Satisfaction, and Meaning

By Wesley Young

Beautiful Savage
Wesley Young

This book is divided into two parts. The first half is a work of fiction. Names, characters, places, historical events, and incidents are either products of the author's imagination or are used fictitiously. Some people referenced in this work exist, but they are portrayed fictitiously and have been altered, relocated, or modified through creative license. Any resemblance of other characters to actual persons, living or dead, is entirely coincidental.

The self-help and development content included in this book is intended for informational and inspirational purposes only. It does not constitute professional, legal, medical, psychological, or financial advice. Readers should consult qualified professionals when necessary.

Published by:

** USA **

ISBN: 979-8-9942327-0-5
Library of Congress Control Number: 2025926845

Cover Design: Vila Design

"Part fable, part life manifesto, *Beautiful Savage* offers a blueprint for those who refuse to choose between security and adventure. A guide for living untamed by convention yet wise in your choices—with the freedom of a savage and the intention of a sage."

—Dr. John Branch,
entrepreneur, Founder,
Texas Vision, inventor of
Virtual Lens

"Ripe with wisdom. *Beautiful Savage* is immeasurably sage. The style is whimsical, the principles are life changing. Wes writes with a voice of clarity and conviction. Want to bridge the gap between your goals and desires? Look no further. Wes and Randy give you the blueprint."

—Randy Marshall,
speaker, author of
Surprised by Serenity

Table of Contents

Foreword

What an honor it is to be asked to write some thoughts on this wisdom-packed story, created by an ever-seeking individual of greater significance. When someone like Wes Young puts pen to paper, you don't just read—you *learn*, you *laugh*, and somewhere in the middle, you start questioning whether you've been living up to your full potential or just making to-do lists about it.

I've had the joy of calling Wes a friend and walking alongside him on this journey of forward motion for the last fifteen years. To be honest, though, his story was already on a strong trajectory before we ever connected. He didn't need me to steer him in the right direction—he was already halfway down the road with the gas pedal pressed to the floor and the GPS in constant "recalculating" mode.

Wes hit life's jackpot when he married an incredible woman who matches him stride for stride—equal parts compassion, grit, and good sense (the kind that keeps someone like Wes balanced). Together they've raised two great kids, both reflections of their parents' curiosity, energy, and knack for asking big questions at the exact moment you're trying to relax. I've loved every moment I've had around their family—almost as much as I've enjoyed time with Wes himself, and that's saying something.

Entrepreneurship seems to be in Wes's DNA. From starting businesses early on and roping in his friends to join the adventure, to his short stint as an electrician, he's always been wired for discovery—pun very much intended. Eventually, he found his ideal career path as a financial advisor, where his ability to connect, inspire, and strategize quickly set him apart. Before long, Wes was leading from the front, consistently ranking in the top five in financial planning out of thousands of advisors. Not bad for a guy who started out with only a toolbox and a dream.

The journey you're about to embark on through this fable beautifully illustrates the impact of wisdom intersecting with our life's path. Wes is a man on a mission—to close his gap, increase his fuel, expand his faith, and step more boldly into significance. This story isn't just a reflection of that pursuit; it's an open invitation to join him in it. You'll laugh, you'll think, and somewhere along the way, you might even start taking inventory of your own journey—where you've grown, and where maybe you've been coasting in neutral.

I've been blessed myself to have wise, spiritually grounded individuals cross my path—people who didn't just tell me what I *wanted* to hear, but what I *needed* to hear. Decades later, their influence still echoes in my heart. After reading this story, I found myself freshly inspired to seek out the next wise voice to guide me—or at least to remind me that the path to growth usually includes a few bumps, potholes, and maybe a flat tire or two.

Before I wrap up this foreword, I want to highlight something that resonated deeply with me—Wes's encouragement to *seek resistance*. In today's world, that sounds borderline ridiculous, doesn't it? We've become a culture obsessed with shortcuts, comfort zones, and avoiding anything that requires breaking a sweat—physical or emotional. We're told life should be easy, effortless, and if it's hard, you must be doing it wrong. But as Wes points out, the *struggle* is often the secret ingredient to significance.

"Go for hard." On the surface, that sounds like a line from a motivational poster hung in a CrossFit gym. But look deeper, and it hits at the core of spiritual and personal development. It brings me back to one of my favorite (and most challenging) Bible verses: James 1:2—"Consider it pure joy, my brothers and sisters, whenever you face trials of many kinds, because the testing of your faith develops perseverance."

Consider it *joy* when things fall apart? That's not human nature—that's divine wisdom. It takes a confident, faith-filled, purpose-driven person to look at breakdown and say, "Well, this must be where the breakthrough's hiding." Failure, as Wes reminds us, isn't final—it's feedback. If you aren't failing occasionally, you probably aren't stretching far enough.

So buckle up. The story you're about to read isn't just a fable; it's an invitation to grow. It's a mirror reflecting both who you are and who you could become if you dare to lean into resistance, faith, and purpose. I hope you enjoy every lesson, every laugh, and every uncomfortable truth tucked inside these pages as much as I did.

Because if there's one thing Wes has taught me, it's this: Life's too short to play it safe—and far too meaningful not to play it *significant*.

Michael Scovel
New York Life Managing Partner,
Dallas, Texas

Introduction

The Entrepreneur's Paradox

You've felt it, haven't you? That tension between being told to "be grateful for what you have" and the burning desire to build something better. The guilt that comes with wanting more when you already have so much. The exhaustion of defending your drive to people who think you should just "slow down and smell the roses."

Here's what they don't understand: **Ambition IS CRITICAL to contentment**. Not the enemy of it.

The gap between where you are and where you want to be isn't a character flaw to be fixed—it's the source of your aliveness. The resistance you face isn't something to merely endure—it's what makes victory sweet. The battle isn't what you have to get through to find happiness—the battle IS where happiness lives.

This book is your manifesto. It's permission to be fully yourself without apology. It's a framework for loving the fight while winning the war.

Welcome to the Beautiful Savage way of life.

How to Use This Book

This book is designed to serve different types of readers and learning styles. It's structured in two complementary parts that work together to transform how you think about entrepreneurship, success, and fulfillment.

Part I: The Beautiful Savage Fable

A supernatural story of mentorship and transformation.

If you learn best through stories, start here. This short fable follows Wes, a struggling young entrepreneur, as he encounters Randy Marshall, a mysterious mentor who teaches him the Beautiful Savage principles through fishing lessons on Lake Travis.

Part II: The Beautiful Savage Framework

The comprehensive business and life system.

This is the core content—the proven framework for integrating big ambition, grateful condition, and savage persistence into a life of meaning, enjoyment, and satisfaction. You'll get the practical tools, systematic approaches, and actionable strategies that have helped hundreds of entrepreneurs build successful companies while living with joy.

Part I

The Beautiful Savage Fable

A supernatural tale of mentorship, transformation,
and divine purpose.

Chapter 1

The Meeting at Dawn

The morning mist hung low over Lake Travis as Wes adjusted his tackle box for the third time. At twenty-three, with a wife and two young kids at home, every fishing trip felt stolen from the mountain of responsibilities waiting for him. He'd been trying to build a financial strategy company for months, but clients were scarce and bills were mounting. Today felt different though, partly because of the old man sitting on the dock about fifty yards downstream.

Randy looked to be in his seventies, his weathered hands working a fly rod with the kind of precision that only comes from decades of practice. What caught Wes's attention wasn't just the old man's skill, but the pile of impressive bass lying in his cooler—fish that dwarfed anything Wes had ever caught. Despite his unassuming appearance in worn jeans and a simple fishing shirt, there was something about Randy's quiet confidence that suggested depths beneath the surface.

"Excuse me," Wes called out as he approached. "I've been fishing this lake for months and haven't caught anything close to what you've got there. What's your secret?"

Randy looked up with eyes that seemed to hold both kindness and mischief. "Son, fishing ain't just about the gear or even knowing where the fish are. It's about understanding the gap."

"The gap?"

"The space between where you are and where you want to be. Most folks either get frustrated by that gap or try to ignore it. But that gap? That's where all the good stuff happens."

Randy gestured to the empty spot on the dock beside him. "Got time for a story?"

As Randy spoke, he lifted his latest catch from the water—a beautiful bass with one distinctive feature that made Wes lean forward. The fish was missing its right fin, and its left fin was completely black.

"Would you look at that," Randy said with a knowing smile, holding the unique fish up for Wes to see clearly. "Sometimes the most beautiful things are the ones that are different, marked by their journey."

Randy locked eyes with Wes as he continued to hold the fish. "Remember this fish, Wes. I mean really remember it. Study those markings. One day, this might mean a lot to you—more than you can imagine right now."

He gently released the fish back into the lake, watching as it swam away with strong, purposeful strokes. "You might see it again someday, son. And when you do, you'll understand why this moment mattered."

Chapter 2

The Gap

As Wes settled onto the weathered planks, Randy continued working his line with practiced ease.

"When I was about your age—maybe a little younger—I had this idea that I was gonna build something meaningful. Problem was, I didn't even know what that looked like yet." Randy chuckled. "Sounds like you might understand that feeling."

Wes shifted uncomfortably. How could this stranger know about his struggles? "I'm trying to build a financial strategy company, but it's . . . harder than I expected."

"Two young kids at home?"

"How did you—" Wes started, then stopped. "Yes. And a wife who believes in what I'm building, even when I have doubts myself."

Randy nodded knowingly. "Well, I had this gap, see? Between where I was—which was basically a guy with good intentions and big dreams —and where I wanted to be, which was actually successful enough to provide for my family. Most people try to close that gap as fast as possible, or they get discouraged and quit."

Randy paused to set the hook on another bass. As he fought the fish, he continued. "But I learned something important: That gap ain't your enemy. It's your fuel."

"Fuel?"

"Yep. See, I realized that gap was always gonna be there. Soon as I got good at serving one family, I wanted to serve ten families. When I finally had ten clients, I started dreaming about building a team. The gap just moves."

Randy netted the fish—another beautiful bass that would have been Wes's personal best. "The trick is learning to love the gap. To see it as sacred. Because without it, you're just going through the motions."

Wes watched the old man release the fish back into the lake. "Why'd you let it go?"

"Because I already caught what I came for today. Sometimes the catching matters, sometimes it don't. What always matters is staying in the game." Randy looked directly at Wes. "Your gap with your business? That's sacred territory, son. That's where faith lives."

The words hit Wes like a revelation. "Faith?"

"This is where faith lives. Faith is the substance of things hoped for, the evidence of things not yet seen. Without faith, it's impossible to please God, because God made us to have big faith in a future that we cannot yet see, but we can hope for."

Randy's voice took on the cadence of someone who'd spent years in pulpits. "I used to preach this every Sunday—this gap ain't your enemy, it's your fuel. It's what drives us to become more than we are. You know what Saint Irenaeus said? 'The glory of God is man fully alive.' That gap you're feeling, that restlessness to build something meaningful? That's you coming alive, son. That's you becoming who God designed you to be."

"You were a preacher?"

"Still am, in a way. Just different pulpits now." Randy began packing up his gear with movements that seemed almost ethereal. "Listen, Wes—and yeah, I know your name, just like I know you're gonna figure this out. The company you're trying to build? It's not just about financial strategy. It's about helping families steward what God's entrusted to them. Keep that in mind."

As Randy walked away, Wes realized he'd never told the man his name. By the time he turned around, Randy had disappeared completely, leaving only wet footprints on the dock that seemed to evaporate in the morning sun.

Chapter 3

Making New Normal

Two weeks passed before Wes returned to Lake Travis. His business struggles had intensified—another potential client had chosen a larger firm—but his wife, Jamie, remained his strongest supporter, continuing to encourage him to pursue his vision even when the path seemed uncertain. He needed the peace of the water to think through his next moves.

To his surprise, Randy was in the same spot, but this time the old man was using completely different gear and a technique Wes had never seen before.

"Different setup today?" Wes asked, relieved to see the mysterious mentor again.

Randy nodded without looking up from his intricate knot-tying. "Drop-shot rig. Been wanting to try this for months but kept putting it off because I was comfortable with what I knew."

"Is it working?"

"Don't know yet. That's the point." Randy cast out the unfamiliar rig with obvious uncertainty. "See, Wes, we all got what I call our 'normal.' It's how we do things. For you, that might be relying on the same network of people you knew before you came into this business."

"How do you know about—"

"You were an electrician, right?" Randy smiled mysteriously. "Great framework for starting out in the financial services business. You know a lot of people, they like you. How's that working for you?"

Wes shifted uncomfortably. "It's . . . okay. But I'm starting to run out of people I know well enough to approach."

"Exactly. There are clients out there you can't reach with your normal methods. But learning new approaches? It's clunky. You're terrible at it right now."

As if to prove his point, Randy's cast tangled in some weeds. He patiently worked it free.

"This is what I call 'normalizing new,'" he continued. "Taking something that requires all your conscious attention and doing it enough times that it becomes automatic. Like when you first learned to drive—remember how hard that was? Now you don't even think about it."

"How long does it take?"

"Ain't about time, son. It's about iterations. How many times are you willing to do something poorly before you do it well?" Randy made another cast, this one clean and precise. "The gravitational pull is always toward what you already know. But growth lives in the space between what you can do and what you can't do yet."

Over the next hour, Wes watched Randy's technique improve with each cast. By the end of the morning, the old man had caught three fish using the new method.

"Now I've got two ways to fish Lake Travis instead of one," Randy said with satisfaction. "And next week, I'll try something else new."

"You know," Randy said, settling back on the dock, "Jesus told a story that perfectly illustrates what we're talking about. A master gave three servants different amounts of money before leaving on a journey. Two servants took risks, invested their talents, and doubled their money. The third servant played it safe, buried his talent, and returned only what he was given."

Randy's voice took on that preacher's cadence again. "When the master returned, he celebrated the two who had taken risks: 'Well done, good and faithful servant! You have been faithful with a few things; I will put you in charge of many things.'

"But to the servant who played it safe, he said, 'You wicked, lazy servant! You should have at least put my money on deposit with the bankers.'"

Randy looked directly at Wes. "Notice what happened: The servants who 'normalized new'—who took their talents from the safe, familiar approach to a new, risky approach—were rewarded with greater responsibility and opportunity. The servant who defended his normal approach was condemned for it.

"The gravitational pull is always toward burying your talents." Randy's eyes seemed to see right through Wes. "It's safer. It's predictable. You can't lose what you were given. But Jesus is clear: Playing it safe with what you've been entrusted with isn't faithfulness—it's faithlessness.

"Your talents—your abilities, your vision for helping families, your drive to build something meaningful—they're not given to you to maintain, Wes. They're given to you to multiply. And multiplication requires normalizing new."

When Wes looked up from processing these words, Randy was gone again. Only the wet outline of where he'd been sitting remained, already fading in the Texas sun.

Chapter 4

Allocating Energy

A month later, Wes arrived at Lake Travis to find Randy organizing an impressive array of equipment—multiple rods, tackle boxes sorted by technique, and what looked like a detailed map of the lake.

"Big plans today?" Wes asked, no longer surprised by Randy's sudden appearances.

"Nope. Big plans for the season." Randy spread out the map, which was covered in pencil marks, depth notations, and seasonal patterns. "See, I've been thinking about energy—and I've been watching how you're approaching your business."

"Energy?"

"Every day you go out there trying to build your company, you've got limited energy. The question is how much do you spend on what you already know versus learning something new?"

Randy pointed to different sections of the map. "Early in the season, when I was learning Lake Travis, maybe 75 percent of my energy went to trying new spots, new techniques, figuring out patterns. Only 25 percent was just fishing what I knew worked."

"That sounds exhausting."

"It was! Progress was slow. But then I started to normalize some of that new stuff, and I could shift to maybe 50-50. Then when I really got rolling, I was spending 75 percent of my energy on what I knew worked and only 25 percent on new stuff."

Randy rolled up the map. "But here's the trap, Wes. If I stay at that 75 percent normal, 25 percent new forever, I plateau. The fish get wise to my patterns, conditions change, and suddenly what used to work stops working."

"So what do you do?"

"Every few months, I force myself back to 50-50. Sometimes even back to 75 percent new again. It's uncomfortable, but it's how you keep growing.

"The parable of the talents reveals something profound about energy allocation," Randy continued. "The two faithful servants didn't just work harder with what they had—they allocated their energy differently. They moved from the normal—safe storage—to new—risky investment.

"The third servant represents what happens when you stay stuck at 100 percent normal, 0 percent new. He expended energy on preservation rather than multiplication. He was busy but not productive. He was active but not growing."

Randy picked up a technique he'd never used before—a complex Carolina rig setup. "Jesus is teaching us that faithful stewardship requires the courage to risk what you have to gain what you could have. This is the essence of the energy allocation model—constantly cycling between the security of proven systems and the risk of unproven opportunities.

"The master's response reveals the principle: 'To those who have, more will be given.' This isn't about favoritism—it's about the compound effect of consistently choosing growth over safety, new over normal.

"The third servant's fate is a warning: When you refuse to allocate energy toward new possibilities, you don't just stay the same—you eventually lose what you had. 'Take the bag of gold from him and give it to the one who has ten bags.'"

Randy made a practice cast with the new setup. "This is why the energy allocation model isn't optional for Beautiful Savages—it's biblical stewardship in action.

"Today's a 75 percent new day for me. I might not catch much, but I'll learn something that helps me catch more later."

As they fished, Randy explained how this principle applied to everything—Wes's financial planning business that he'd built to serve clients across the country, learning new technology to better serve his remote team, even his relationships. "The energy allocation model works everywhere, son. Question is: Are you brave enough to feel clunky again?"

When Wes turned to respond, Randy had vanished once more, leaving only the gentle ripples where his line had been.

Chapter 5

The Greatest Moments

It was early fall when Wes next encountered Randy, but this time the old man wasn't fishing. He was sitting on the dock with a worn leather journal, writing intently.

"Taking a break from fishing?" Wes asked. His business had begun to turn around—he'd implemented several of Randy's suggestions and was starting to see real results.

Randy looked up and smiled. "Actually, I'm doing my quarterly review. Every three months, I sit down and think about the best moments from the previous season."

"You mean like the biggest fish you caught?"

"That's part of it." Randy flipped through pages filled with detailed notes and small sketches. "But it's more than that. I write down all the great moments—the times I figured out a new pattern, that morning when everything clicked with a difficult technique, the satisfaction of helping someone understand something important."

Wes sat down beside him. "Why?"

"Two reasons. First, it fills me with gratitude. I look at all this and realize how rich my life is, how much I've learned, how many great experiences I've had."

Randy turned to a page covered with photos taped into the journal—pictures of fish, sunrises, and what appeared to be various people in different settings.

"But the second reason is even more important," Randy continued. "It gives me confidence for what I'm capable of next. Look here—three months ago, I wrote down that I wanted to learn a completely new approach to deep-water fishing. I was terrible at it, frustrated, ready to quit a dozen times."

He flipped to a recent entry with a photo of a beautiful bass. "But here I am, catching fish using methods I never thought I'd master. If I can do that, what else am I capable of?"

"So it's not just about being grateful?"

"Grateful condition ain't passive, son. It's strategic. When you regularly remind yourself of what you've accomplished, what you've overcome, what you've enjoyed—it fuels your capacity for the next big jump."

Randy closed the journal and looked out over Lake Travis. "Most people focus so hard on where they're going, they don't enjoy where they are on the way to where they're going. And they'll be going somewhere for the rest of their lives."

"That sounds exhausting."

"Only if you forget to count your blessings along the way. But when you do this regular audit, something beautiful happens—you realize you're living an extraordinary life, even in the middle of chasing bigger dreams."

Randy began to fade like the morning mist, his voice becoming softer. "Wes, start keeping your own journal. Record your greatest moments—in business, with your family, in your growth. You'll be amazed at what you discover about yourself."

Chapter 6

Resistance

Winter had arrived, and Lake Travis was quieter with the cooler weather keeping most anglers away. Wes found Randy in his workshop—though Wes had never seen this workshop before and couldn't quite remember how he'd gotten there. The old man was working on lures for the coming season, his hands moving with practiced precision, but Wes could see several discarded attempts scattered around the workbench.

"Tough project?" Wes asked.

Randy held up a half-finished lure. "I'm trying to create something I've never made before—a lure that'll work in conditions I've never fished. It's harder than I expected."

"What's the problem?"

"The problem?" Randy laughed. "The problem is resistance, son. And resistance comes in three flavors."

Randy set down his tools and faced Wes. "First is fear. I'm scared this new design won't work. Scared I'll waste materials, waste time, look foolish when I try it out on the water."

"That makes sense."

"Second is fatigue. Learning new things is exhausting. It'd be so much easier to just make the same lures I've always made. They work fine. Why complicate things?"

Randy picked up one of the discarded attempts. "And third is arrogance. Part of me thinks, 'Randy, you've been making lures for forty years. You know what works. Why are you listening to some young guide who suggested this crazy design?'"

"So how do you deal with it?"

Randy smiled. "You dance with it. See, resistance ain't your enemy—it's confirmation that you're doing something important. If there's no resistance, you're probably not growing."

"Dancing sounds peaceful. This looks frustrating."

"Dancing can be frustrating, too, if you don't know the steps." Randy picked up his tools again. "For fear, I need faith. I remember all the times I've tried new things before and they worked out. I remind myself why I'm doing this—to become a more complete angler."

"What about fatigue?"

"For fatigue, I need what I call savage persistence. I schedule this work when my energy is highest. I break it into small pieces. And I iterate—try something, see how it works, adjust, try again."

"And arrogance?"

Randy paused thoughtfully. "For arrogance, I need humility. I have to remember that I don't know everything, that conditions change, that there's always someone who knows something I don't. That young guide? He's fishing conditions I've never faced. Maybe I should listen."

Randy returned to his work, his movements more confident now. "The beautiful thing about resistance is that on the other side of it lives the most beautiful, savage version of yourself."

The workshop began to shimmer and fade, and Wes found himself standing alone by the lake, not entirely sure how he'd gotten there.

Chapter 7

Face Everything and Rise

Spring had returned, and Wes met Randy at a new location—a remote spot on Lake Travis that required a challenging hike to reach. His business was thriving now—he'd landed several major clients and was considering hiring his first team member. But Randy had insisted on making this trek.

"Why here?" Wes asked as they caught their breath.

"Because you're scared of it," Randy replied matter-of-factly. "This spot is supposed to have the biggest bass on the lake, but it's difficult to reach, unfamiliar water, and requires techniques you're not comfortable with."

As they fished, Randy shared his philosophy about fear. "There's a difference between experiencing the emotion of fear and being afraid, son. Fear is information. Being afraid is limitation."

"I'm not sure I follow."

"Well, you're experiencing fear right now about hiring that first employee. Will they work out? Can you afford them? What if you can't provide enough work? What if they're better than you?"

Randy paused to adjust his setup. "But you're not going to be afraid. You're going to face everything and rise."

"Is that from something?"

"Jesus was constantly telling his disciples, 'Don't be afraid.' But notice, he wasn't putting them in safe situations. He was constantly putting them in environments where they'd experience fear. The difference is you can feel the emotion without taking on the identity."

Randy's voice carried the authority of someone who'd spent decades studying these truths. "I preached this for twenty years before I really understood it myself—courage isn't the absence of fear, it's faith in action."

They reached a particularly challenging pool, and Randy began working it with techniques Wes had never seen.

"Now I'm really scared," Randy admitted with a grin, "which means I'm exactly where I need to be."

Over the next several hours, Wes watched Randy work through his uncertainty systematically. Each failed attempt was followed by analysis and adjustment. Each moment of doubt was countered with reminders of past successes.

"Fear is like taking a trip with your crazy uncle," Randy said as he worked the pool. "You let him come on the trip, but you don't let him drive."

When Randy finally connected with a massive bass—the biggest either of them had ever seen—his joy was infectious.

"See that?" he said as he released the fish. "On the other side of that fear was the most beautiful, savage version of myself. The version that could try new techniques and catch the fish of a lifetime."

Randy looked directly at Wes. "And on the other side of your fear about hiring that team member is the version of yourself that can build something bigger than you ever imagined."

As they packed up, Randy seemed to become translucent in the evening light. "Hire Jamie first," he said with a knowing smile. "She's been wanting to join the business anyway."

Wes blinked, and Randy was gone. But the advice proved prophetic—his wife, Jamie, became his first and best business partner.

Chapter 8

The Energy Thief

Summer brought its own challenges. Wes found Randy looking unusually tired, sitting on their familiar dock with his gear mostly untouched. The business was scaling rapidly now—they had a small team and clients across three states.

"Everything okay?" Wes asked.

Randy sighed. "Just fighting the energy thief."

"The what?"

"Fatigue, son. See, you've been so excited about all the growth in your business, all the new systems you want to implement, all the markets you want to enter. But change is exhausting."

Randy gestured to his tackle box, which was more organized than Wes had ever seen. "Change is like remodeling a house while you're trying to live in it. It's messy, inconvenient, and actually less effective initially than if you just left everything alone."

"So what do you do?"

"You get systematic about it. You can't just hope you'll have energy for new things. You have to schedule them first, when your energy is the highest."

Randy pulled out a simple notebook with his weekly schedule. "See here? Tuesday mornings are for trying new techniques. Thursday evenings are for maintaining gear. Saturday early is for exploring new water."

"That seems rigid."

"Structure creates freedom, son. When I don't have a system, fatigue makes a coward of me. I end up doing the same old things because they're easy, even when I know they won't get me to where I want to go."

Randy opened his tackle box and began preparing a setup Wes had never seen before. "The gravitational pull is always toward the normal. But if you don't regularly put energy toward new, you stagnate. Eventually, you decline."

"How do you know what new things to focus on?"

"Good question. That's where the activity matrix comes in. Every three months, I list everything I currently do, then I ask: What new activities would move the needle most? What old activities should I delegate or delete?"

Randy cast out his new setup with obvious intention. "Today I'm deleting my old approach to this deep-water structure and trying something completely different. It might not work, but doing the same thing that's not working isn't working either."

As if to validate his point, Randy hooked into a fish almost immediately.

"Sometimes the energy spent on new pays off right away," he said with a smile as he fought the fish. "Sometimes it takes months. But it always pays off eventually."

Randy's form began to waver like heat shimmer. "Remember, Wes— you can't do everything, but you can do a few things that will move the needle the most in a 90-day period. The inspiration is the deadline."

Chapter 9

Success-Induced Blindness

It was late in the season when Wes arrived to find Randy struggling with something he'd never seen before—the old man was having a bad day on the water. Multiple equipment failures, missed strikes, and what looked like genuine frustration. Wes's company now had offices in five states and was being recognized as a leader in its market.

"Rough morning?" Wes asked carefully.

Randy sat down heavily on the dock. "Worse than rough. I've been using the same approaches that made me successful all season, and suddenly nothing's working. Reminds me of something I learned in ministry."

"How so?"

"There was a time when I got so comfortable with certain sermon styles, certain ways of connecting with the congregation, that I stopped listening for what God was actually calling me to say. I was preaching what worked before, not what was needed now."

"Maybe it's just an off day?"

"Maybe. Or maybe I'm falling into the trap I've seen destroy more good anglers than anything else—same trap that almost ended my ministry years ago." Randy looked out over the lake with a mixture of frustration and self-awareness. "Success-induced blindness."

"What do you mean?"

"When you've had success with certain methods, it's easy to start believing your way is the best way. You point to your results and say, 'Look how well I'm doing. Why would I change?'"

Randy pulled out his journal and flipped to entries from earlier in the season—pages filled with successful outings and trophy fish. "See all this? This is dangerous."

"Your success is dangerous?"

"My attachment to it is. When I start thinking I've got it all figured out, I stop looking for new information. I stop being humble. I stop growing."

Randy told Wes about a guide he used to know—one of the best on the lake for years. "He had this system that worked perfectly for about five years. Caught fish when nobody else could. But he got so invested in being right about his methods that he stopped adapting when conditions changed."

"What happened to him?"

"The lake changed. New fishing pressure, different weather patterns, evolving fish behavior. His old methods stopped working, but he kept using them because they'd always worked before. Last I heard, he was barely catching anything."

Randy stood up and switched to completely different gear. "The antidote to arrogance is humility. I have to remember that I don't know everything, that conditions change, that there's always someone who knows something I don't. Same lesson God taught me when I was getting too comfortable in the pulpit."

"So you're starting over?"

"Not starting over. Starting fresh. Big difference." Randy made a cast with the new setup. "Proverbs says, 'Pride comes before the fall, but humility brings wisdom.' Everything I learned before still matters. But I can't let what I know prevent me from learning what I don't know."

Within an hour, Randy had adapted to the changing conditions and was catching fish again. "Pride comes before the fall, son. But humility? Humility keeps you in the game. That's not just fishing wisdom—that's Kingdom wisdom."

Randy began to shimmer in the afternoon light. "Don't let your success become your limitation, Wes. You're about to enter a phase where everything you've built could blind you to what you need to build next."

Chapter 10

The Beautiful Savage Rhythm

As autumn painted the trees around Lake Travis, Wes found Randy in a familiar scene—sitting on the dock with his journal, but this time surrounded by gear that represented an entire season of growth and learning. Wes's company was now a multimillion-dollar operation with team members across the country.

"End of season review time?" Wes asked.

"End of season review," Randy confirmed. "Time to put it all together."

Randy opened his journal to reveal a systematic approach that had evolved over their encounters. "See, being a Beautiful Savage ain't about just having big dreams or just being grateful or just being persistent. It's about integrating all three into a rhythm."

"How do you mean?"

Randy pointed to different sections of his journal. "Every ninety days, I do this complete cycle. First, I update my big ambition—where do I want to be in the next three years? What new skills do I want to develop? What experiences do I want to have?"

He flipped through pages covered with photos and detailed notes. "Then I refresh my grateful condition. I go through all the great moments from the past quarter, remember how far I've come, to build confidence for what I'm capable of next."

"And then?"

"Then I assess my resistance. What form is it taking right now? Fear of new techniques? Fatigue from too much change? Arrogance from recent success? And I apply the right antidote."

Randy closed the journal and looked at Wes seriously. "But here's the key, son. Then, I take action. All the planning in the world don't mean nothing if you don't get out on the water."

"It sounds like a lot of work."

"It is work. But it's joyful work. See, most people think you have to choose between being driven and being happy. Between wanting more and being grateful. Between pushing hard and enjoying the journey."

Randy gestured to the lake, where the setting sun was creating a perfect mirror on the water. "But that's a false choice. The Beautiful Savage way is about integrating all three macronutrients of happiness right into the pursuit itself."

"The three what?"

"The three macronutrients of happiness. Think about it. Remember last year when you worked with that trainer?" Wes had given up trying to guess how Randy knew things about him they had never discussed. "What did he have you track on your fancy phone? Macros. Protein, fat, and carbs, right? Well just like there are three macronutrients to getting in better shape, there are three macronutrients to happiness. Enjoyment, satisfaction, and meaning. Meaning through big ambitions that serve others. Enjoyment through grateful reflection on the journey. Satisfaction through persistent engagement with worthy resistance."

Randy stood and began packing his gear with efficient movements. "You don't have to apologize for wanting to build something bigger, Wes. God designed you to grow, to want more, to become more. You don't have to choose between loving what you have and building something better."

"So what's the secret?"

Randy looked directly at Wes, and for a moment, Wes could see the preacher Randy used to be—and still was. "Love the battle. Live with joy. Dance with the resistance between where you are and where you want to be. Because on the other side of that resistance lives the most beautiful, savage version of yourself—the version God always intended."

Randy paused at the edge of the dock. "This is our last meeting like this, son. You've learned what you need to learn. Now you need to live it."

"Will I see you again?"

Randy smiled mysteriously. "You'll see me again, son. But be a Beautiful Savage right now. Have a big ambition, a grateful condition, and a savage persistence to navigate the resistance between the life you're living and the unlived life within you."

Randy looked out over the lake, then back at Wes. "Look at this lake, son. Think about everything we've talked about. You'll see my footprints up the stairs and maybe something else I will leave you. I love you and believe in you. God has a great plan and purpose for your life. Remember that!"

Randy removed his worn sandals. "And remember—I may want these back later." He set them carefully on the dock with a knowing smile.

With that, Randy Marshall walked barefoot into the evening mist and disappeared, leaving Wes alone with twenty-five years of building ahead of him—and a pair of weathered sandals that somehow felt like a promise.

Wes looked around, trying to process what had just happened. All he could see were wet footprints leading up the stairs from the dock, already beginning to fade in the evening air.

Chapter 11

The Gathering—Twenty-Five Years Later

The evening air was perfect on Wes's deck overlooking Lake Travis. At forty-eight, he had built exactly what he'd dreamed of all those years ago—a thriving financial strategy company with clients and team members across the country. Tonight, he was celebrating with four of his closest friends, each nursing a glass of Spring Mountain Cabernet as they watched the sunset paint the water gold.

"Hard to believe we've all ended up in Austin," said Mike, checking his expensive watch in the casual setting. As a senior executive with one of the largest insurance companies in the country, Mike's success was evident in everything from his impeccable style to his genuine care for others. He was the friend who had taken Wes shopping for clothes that were actually in style.

"Speak for yourself." Dev laughed, the picture of relaxed success. His business development and mergers and acquisitions firm had made him wealthy beyond measure, but more importantly, he'd maintained his values throughout the climb. "I moved here because Wes wouldn't stop talking about this lake."

John, quieter but no less accomplished, swirled his wine thoughtfully. The ophthalmologist had built multiple surgery centers and accumulated substantial real estate holdings, but his crowning achievement was the virtual lens technology he'd invented—a revolutionary system that changed how people selected eyeglasses, contact lenses, and lenses for lens replacement surgery. The company had sold for hundreds of millions, but John wore his success lightly.

Barry, athletic and energetic despite being in his late forties, stretched back in his chair with the easy confidence of someone who'd built and rebuilt success multiple times. Over the years, he'd acquired, improved, and sold several apparel companies and fitness equipment manufacturers. His ability to see potential in struggling businesses and transform them into market leaders had made him wealthy, but more than that, it had given him a reputation as someone who could turn any venture around.

"You know what's funny?" Wes said, looking out over the water where he'd spent so many transformative mornings decades ago. "I've been thinking lately about this old man I used to meet down at the lake when I was just starting out. Taught me everything I know about business, really. His name was Randy Marshall."

Mike nearly choked on his wine. "Did you say Randy Marshall?"

"Yeah, why?"

"Older guy? Weathered hands? Talked about gaps and resistance and something called 'Beautiful Savage'?"

Wes sat up straighter. "You knew Randy?"

"Knew him?" Dev set down his glass with a look of amazement. "He's the reason I'm sitting here. I met him during the worst period of my life—my first business had failed, I was drowning in debt, and I was about ready to give up on everything."

John was staring at all of them with wide eyes. "This is impossible. Randy Marshall mentored me too, but that was fifteen years ago when I was struggling to get my first surgery center approved. He appeared out of nowhere, taught me about persistence and faith, and then . . ."

Barry sat forward suddenly, his face pale. "Wait a minute. Are you guys talking about an old fisherman who smelled like Old Spice and had this way of just . . . knowing things he shouldn't know?"

"And then he disappeared," all five men said simultaneously.

They sat in stunned silence for several minutes, each processing the implications.

"He taught you about the three forms of resistance?" Wes asked.

"Fear, fatigue, and arrogance," Mike replied immediately. "And their antidotes—faith, systematic action, and humility."

"Big ambition, grateful condition, savage persistence," Dev added. "The three macronutrients of happiness through enjoyment, satisfaction, and meaning."

"The energy allocation model," John contributed. "Cycling between normal and new to avoid plateau."

Barry shook his head in disbelief. "He taught me about seeing potential in broken things. Said most people look at a failing business and see problems, but Beautiful Savages see opportunities. That's how I learned to find diamonds in the rough."

As they compared notes, the parallels in their stories became undeniable. Each had met Randy during a crucial period of struggle. Each had been taught the same principles. Each had experienced the mysterious way Randy would appear and disappear. And somehow, all five had become close friends over the years without ever realizing their connection to the same mentor.

"Wait," Dev said, starting to laugh despite the impossibility of it all. "Did he always smell like Old Spice?"

"Yes!" Mike exclaimed. "I thought that was just me noticing that. Classic Old Spice, like he'd been wearing it since 1975."

"Same here," John added with a grin. "I used to think it was funny—this wise mentor who smelled like my grandfather."

Barry nodded emphatically. "That and he always had this way of disappearing right when you needed to process what he'd just taught you."

Wes shook his head in amazement. "Even that detail is the same. What are the odds?"

"Gentlemen," came a familiar voice from the edge of the deck.

They turned to see Randy Marshall stepping into the light—looking exactly the same as he had twenty-five years ago. Not a day older, same weathered hands, same knowing eyes, same humble demeanor.

The five successful men sat speechless.

"Don't look so shocked," Randy said with that familiar chuckle, settling into an empty chair as if he'd been invited. "Did you really think those encounters were coincidences?"

"How is this possible?" Wes managed to ask.

"How isn't the right question, son. Why is better." Randy looked around at each of them with obvious pride. "Look at what you've built. Look at who you've become."

Randy's gaze lingered on each man. "Wes, you've helped hundreds of families create lasting legacies and build generational wealth. Mike, you've transformed how an entire industry thinks about serving people rather than just selling products. Dev, you've facilitated mergers that created thousands of jobs and brought innovation to markets that needed it. John, your invention has literally changed how millions of people see the world. And Barry, you've breathed new life into dozens of companies and saved thousands of jobs by seeing potential where others saw only problems.

"But here's what makes me most proud," Randy continued, his voice taking on that familiar preacher's cadence. "You've become extraordinary husbands, fathers, sons, and men. You've learned to love the battle while living with joy."

Mike leaned forward. "Randy, we have so many questions—"

"And I'm sure you do. But tonight isn't about the how or the why of my presence. It's about the what's next." Randy stood and walked to the deck railing, looking out over Lake Travis. "See, boys, you might think the story ends here. You've achieved success, built great companies, raised families, impacted communities."

He turned back to face them. "But that's not the end. That's the beginning of the next chapter."

"What do you mean?" Dev asked.

"I mean you've normalized new at the highest levels in business. Now it's time to normalize new at the highest levels of significance." Randy's eyes held that familiar mixture of challenge and encouragement. "You've learned to dance with resistance in building companies. Now learn to dance with it in building a legacy that outlasts you."

Randy moved toward each man, placing a hand on their shoulders. "The gap between where you are and where you want to be? It's still there. It's just moved to a higher level. The resistance you feel toward the next phase of your calling? That's not something to overcome—it's something to dance with."

"What's the next phase?" John asked quietly.

"That's for you to discover together. But I will say this—everything I taught each of you individually was preparation for what you're going to accomplish collectively." Randy smiled at their confused expressions. "Why do you think you all became such close friends? Why do you think you all ended up in the same city? Why do you think you're all sitting here together right now?"

The men exchanged glances, beginning to sense the magnitude of what Randy was suggesting.

"Your individual successes were just the foundation. Now you get to build something together that serves the next generation of dreamers and builders." Randy moved toward the edge of the deck. "Boys, celebrate tonight. Enjoy this moment. Count your blessings and remember how far you've come.

"But tomorrow? Tomorrow you start asking questions: What would we attempt if we knew we couldn't fail? What would we build together if we had unlimited resources and unlimited time?"

Randy paused at the edge of the light. "And remember—you still got two lives. The life you're living, and the unlived life within you. Tonight, those two lives are closer than they've ever been."

"Randy, wait—" Wes called out.

But when they looked again, he was gone. Only the faint scent of lake water and Old Spice lingered in the air.

The five friends sat in stunned silence until Mike finally spoke. "Did that really just happen?"

"We all saw it," Dev said quietly.

"We all lived it," John added.

Barry shook his head. "I've been trying to figure out for twenty years how that man knew exactly what I needed to hear when I needed to hear it."

Wes stood and walked to where Randy had been standing. On the deck railing sat a simple note in handwriting they all recognized: *The Beautiful Savage legacy continues. Dance with the resistance. Love the battle. Live with joy. The best is yet to come.*

Chapter 12

The Sign

The next morning, Wes woke before dawn with an inexplicable urge to return to the lake. Something was calling him back to the dock where it all began.

As he gathered his gear, his eyes fell on the fly rod in the corner—a Christmas gift from Jamie years ago that he'd barely used. He hated fly-fishing. Found it pretentious and unnecessarily complicated. But this morning, something made him grab it along with his regular gear.

The lake was glass-calm in the predawn light. Wes settled onto the same dock where he'd first met Randy twenty-five years ago, his mind still processing the impossible events of the night before. As he arranged his gear, he noticed something that made his heart skip—a pair of weathered sandals sitting exactly where Randy had left them all those years ago, as if they'd been waiting for this moment.

He started with his regular gear, casting familiar lures with familiar techniques. Nothing. After an hour of traditional fishing producing no results, he found himself reaching for the fly rod—and slipping his feet into Randy's old sandals. They fit perfectly.

As Wes stood there in those weathered sandals, he felt something profound. All those years when Randy wasn't around—when he was building his business, raising his family, learning to dance with resistance—he had been walking in the footsteps of greatness. Not just Randy's greatness, but the greatness that comes from understanding what it means to be a Beautiful Savage.

A Beautiful Savage has a big ambition, a grateful condition, and a savage persistence to dance with the resistance between the life they're living and the unlived life within them.

Standing in Randy's sandals, Wes understood now that this wasn't just a philosophy—it was a way of being fully alive. A framework that creates meaning through big ambitions that serve others, enjoyment through grateful reflection on the journey, and satisfaction through persistent engagement with worthy resistance.

He thought about the three macronutrients of happiness that Randy had taught him, the same ones Arthur Brooks wrote about: meaning, enjoyment, and satisfaction. For twenty-five years, Wes had been living proof that the entrepreneurial journey, when properly understood through the Beautiful Savage Framework, naturally delivers all three simultaneously.

Standing in the footsteps of greatness, Wes made his first awkward cast with the fly rod.

"I don't even know what I'm doing," he muttered, fumbling with the unfamiliar setup.

His first cast was terrible. His second, worse. By the fifth cast, he was ready to put the fly rod away and stick with what he knew.

Then, on his sixth attempt, something took the fly with such force it nearly pulled the rod from his hands.

The fight was unlike anything he'd experienced on Lake Travis. The fish had power, intelligence, and determination. For fifteen minutes, Wes battled the bass, his respect for both the fish and the fly-fishing technique growing with each run.

When he finally brought the bass to the net, his heart nearly stopped.

The fish was missing its right fin. Its left fin was completely black.

It was the same fish Randy had shown him twenty-five years ago—or one exactly like it.

As Wes held the beautiful bass, examining its distinctive markings, he felt the presence before he saw it. Randy was standing on the dock behind him, looking exactly as he had the night before, exactly as he had a quarter-century ago.

"Sometimes the most beautiful things are the ones that are different," Randy said quietly, "marked by their journey."

Wes looked up, the fish still in his hands. "The same fish?"

"Does it matter?" Randy asked. "What matters is that you're here. What matters is that you've learned to use tools you once hated. What matters is that you're still willing to be surprised by grace."

Randy knelt beside Wes. "That fish could have been caught by any of a thousand anglers over the years. But it waited for you. On this morning. After that conversation last night. Using equipment you never thought you'd master."

"Why?"

"Because Beautiful Savages recognize signs when they see them. And this is your sign, Wes." Randy's voice held the weight of eternal truth. "The thing you've been resistant to, the thing you thought you couldn't master, the thing that seemed unnecessary—sometimes that's exactly the tool you need for the next phase of your calling."

Wes gently released the fish back into the lake, watching it swim away with strong, purposeful strokes despite its distinctive markings.

When he turned around, Randy was gone.

But this time, Wes wasn't surprised. He understood now that Randy appeared when his guidance was needed and disappeared when the lesson was complete. The supernatural nature of their relationship wasn't the mystery—it was the method.

As the sun broke fully over Lake Travis, Wes sat on the dock with his phone, scrolling through his contacts. Mike, Dev, John, Barry. His four closest friends who, impossibly, shared the same mentor and the same calling.

He started a group text: *Guys, we need to talk. I think I know what our next chapter looks like.*

The responses came immediately.

Mike: *I've been thinking the same thing since last night.*
Dev: *I've already started making a list of what we could accomplish together.*
John: *When do we start?*
Barry: *Count me in. I've got some ideas about companies we could help turn around.*

Wes looked out over the lake where it all began, where Randy Marshall had first taught him about the sacred gap between where he was and where he wanted to be. That gap was still there, just as Randy had promised it would be. It had simply moved to a higher level.

But now he wouldn't have to dance with the resistance alone.

As he packed up his gear, Wes made a mental note to practice more with the fly rod. Something told him he was going to need that particular skill for what was coming next.

The Beautiful Savage legacy was about to enter its next phase.

And for the first time in twenty-five years, Wes Young felt like a beginner again.

Epilogue

The Legacy Continues

Six months later, the five friends had launched what they called the Beautiful Savage Foundation—an organization dedicated to mentoring the next generation of entrepreneurs and leaders. Their combined resources, networks, and hard-won wisdom created opportunities for hundreds of young dreamers to learn the principles Randy had taught them.

Wes brought his expertise in financial strategy and family legacy building. Mike contributed his knowledge of transforming industries through servant leadership. Dev offered his mastery of mergers, acquisitions, and business development. John shared his innovative mindset and real estate acumen. Barry provided his unique ability to see potential in struggling ventures and turn them around.

They met quarterly at Lake Travis, always on the same dock where Wes had first encountered their mysterious mentor. Each gathering began with a "greatest moments audit" where they celebrated what they'd accomplished and who they were becoming. They assessed their resistance—individually and collectively—and planned their next 90-day cycle of growth.

The foundation flourished beyond their wildest dreams. Young entrepreneurs from across the country came to Austin to participate in their programs. The principles of big ambition, grateful condition, and savage persistence spread like wildfire through business schools, churches, and communities.

Barry's turnaround expertise became legendary among their mentees. He had a gift for helping failing startups identify what was broken and rebuild from a position of strength. "Every business failure is just an opportunity in disguise," he would tell the young entrepreneurs. "You just have to learn to see what Randy saw."

But Randy Marshall never appeared to them again as a group.

Instead, he showed up in the lives of the people they mentored—always when the lesson was needed most, always disappearing when the student was ready to teach others. The foundation participants would return from fishing trips or chance encounters with stories that sounded impossibly familiar.

"There was this old man named Randy . . ."

And Wes, Mike, Dev, John, and Barry would just smile and nod, understanding that the Beautiful Savage legacy had taken on a life of its own.

Some called it coincidence. Others called it providence.

They called it exactly what Randy had always said it was: the sacred gap between where you are and where you want to be, where faith meets action, where resistance becomes the pathway to greatness, and where ordinary people discover they were designed for extraordinary things.

The gap never goes away. It just moves to a higher level.

And somewhere on the waters of Lake Travis, a distinctive bass with a missing right fin and a black left fin continues to swim, waiting for the next dreamer who needs to learn that the most beautiful things are often the ones marked by their journey.

Between the life we live and the unlived life within us stands resistance. The Beautiful Savage learns to dance with it—sometimes alone, sometimes with others, but always with faith, always with purpose, and always with joy.

Author's Note

The story you've just read is not fiction in its principles, though the narrative itself is. Randy Marshall represents the mentors, teachers, and divine appointments that appear in our lives exactly when we need them most. The Beautiful Savage Framework he teaches is the foundation for a proven system of integrating big ambition, grateful condition, and savage persistence into a life of meaning, enjoyment, and satisfaction.

Your unlived life is waiting.

Part II
The Beautiful Savage Framework

The comprehensive business and life system.

The Beautiful Savage Identity

Chapter 1

What Is a Beautiful Savage?

Most of us have two lives. The life we live and the unlived life within us.
Between these two stands resistance.

—Steven Pressfield

You're killing yourself to grow your business, but some nights you lie awake wondering if it's all worth it. You've achieved milestones, closed deals, and scaled operations—but real happiness keeps slipping through your fingers. Most entrepreneurs get fragments: a win here, a fun moment there, meaning somewhere down the road. A Beautiful Savage doesn't settle for pieces. They craft a life and business that delivers increased profitability and an improved quality of life not only for them but also for those they serve.

A **Beautiful Savage** has **a big ambition, a grateful condition,** and **a savage persistence** to dance with the resistance between the life they're living and the unlived life within them.

This isn't just a catchy phrase. It's a complete operating system for entrepreneurial fulfillment. The term "Beautiful Savage" captures the essential duality that drives entrepreneurial success—being both refined and relentless, both grateful and ambitious, both strategic and persistent. It's memorable, aspirational, and comprehensive. Most importantly, it gives you an identity to step into rather than just a list of values to remember.

We are all in pursuit of happiness. We want the secrets to it. This framework is perfectly designed around what behavioral social scientist Arthur Brooks calls the three macronutrients of happiness: **enjoyment, satisfaction,** and **meaning**. Arthur teaches a class at Harvard University on the art and science of happiness that has a three-year waiting list. His research reveals that true happiness isn't a feeling—it's a combination of three distinct elements that must be cultivated intentionally.

That beautiful combination of enjoyment, satisfaction, and meaning is what most entrepreneurs overlook. But when you approach your entrepreneurial journey through the Beautiful Savage Framework, you naturally experience all three macronutrients simultaneously. You learn to experience these as an integrated whole, allowing you to make a bigger impact and better decisions while having fewer regrets.

From a grateful condition comes enjoyment—the pleasure, the people, the memories that make your work worthwhile.

From savage persistence comes satisfaction—the pride you earn by overcoming resistance.

From big ambition comes meaning—the faith, the relationships, the work that serves others.

The Beautiful Savage Framework creates a self-reinforcing cycle:

• Your **big ambition** gives you courage to face fear and provides meaning.

• Your **grateful condition** builds confidence for the next challenge and creates enjoyment.

• Your **savage persistence** through resistance creates the satisfaction that comes from earned success.

This framework transcends typical business or self-help advice because it integrates spiritual principles, practical systems, and psychological insights into a comprehensive life philosophy. It's not just about achieving goals—it's about becoming the kind of person who consistently creates meaningful outcomes while enjoying the journey.

Before you read further, pause and discover where you already embody the traits of a Beautiful Savage.

Complete the Beautiful Savage Assessment in the Resources section.

This quick self-check will give you a baseline for your growth and help you notice which areas—big ambition, grateful condition, or savage persistence—are strongest for you right now.

Big Ambition—
Creating Meaning Through Purpose

Chapter 2

The Sacred Gap

Faith is taking the first step even when you don't see the whole staircase.
—Martin Luther King Jr.

Let me take you back to my very first job—the one where I got a real paycheck and taxes came out. I worked at Blockbuster Video. Remember those? I was fifteen years old, made $4.25 an hour (minimum wage at the time), and my extraordinarily difficult and important job was to put the tapes back on the shelf. Tapes were these things we used to watch movies on.

I remember having this thought my first year of work: *When I'm making another dollar an hour, I'm going to be rich.* I thought I was going to have all this extra money. I would look at people a couple of income levels above me and think, *How do you have financial problems? You should be throwing a party. You make so much more money than I do.*

The reason I thought that was because I had a gap between where I was and where I wanted to be. At fifteen, another dollar an hour would get me everything on my list. A funny thing happened years later: I was making a lot more money. Do you think my gap went away? No. In fact, I think it got bigger and more complicated.

We all have a gap between where we are and where we want to be, and the gap never actually goes away. It just moves. When it is healthy, I think it is one of the most beautiful things about people. The fact that we want to make today better than yesterday and tomorrow better than today is a good thing. Of course, it's important to expand on "when it's healthy" because the gap can certainly be unhealthy. For instance, you can be so focused on where you want to go that you don't enjoy where you are, on your way to where you're going. You lack a grateful condition. Also if your gap has an ambition that is completely self-seeking, it will be absent of true meaning and work that matters to others. But as we will continue to unpack in this book, a healthy gap is one of the most beautiful expressions of a life well lived!

This profound reframe turns what could feel like perpetual dissatisfaction into something beautiful and purposeful. By connecting ambition to faith and divine purpose, it elevates goal-setting from a self-help exercise into a spiritual practice.

This is where faith lives. Faith is the substance of things hoped for, the evidence of things not yet seen. Without faith, it's impossible to please God, because God made us to have big faith in a future that we cannot yet see, but we can hope for.

This gap and big ambition are part of the fuel we need to do hard things, to hold out for what we ultimately want instead of settling for what we can have immediately. This is particularly powerful because it gives a practical framework for decision-making in moments of temptation or shortcuts.

As Randy told Wes in the fable, "Most people try to close that gap as fast as possible, or they get discouraged and quit." But taking the time to regularly think about what you want in the future will prevent you from doing life by default, and allow you to do it by design.

The Meaning Macronutrient Connection

What sets a Beautiful Savage apart from other ambitious people? Their big ambition isn't self-centered. It's rooted in faith, family, friends, and work that matters to others. It's rooted in everything that Arthur Brooks discovered about meaning, one of the three macronutrients of happiness. Faith is seeing the future before it's visible and believing it's worth building. Faith gives you the courage to start before you even think you're ready and to stay when it gets hard. And when what you are building lifts up others as well as yourself, you're not just chasing a goal, you're shaping a future that matters.

We can all have a vision for our future that's very self-centered, and we can probably achieve it. Have you ever seen the show *Succession*? Those people had a big vision of where they wanted to go, but it was all about them, and they weren't very happy people. True meaning requires that your ambition extends beyond yourself.

When what you're building has a bigger impact on people other than just you, you tap into something transcendent. Your work becomes worship. Your business becomes mission. Your success becomes service.

Your Big Ambition

How can you identify your current gap? The best way I have found to do this is by writing a draft of your big ambition.

Write down where you want to be in three years in the big areas of life (relational, financial, professional, physical, spiritual). Now imagine you've already arrived there: What does a typical week look like? What happens in a month? What does your full year include? Paint a vivid story that touches all these areas. Don't worry about the how yet—just focus on what an extraordinary life would look like. Also don't design your big ambition (your where you want to be) from your past. While it's important to assess where you are now, it's equally important to design the future as if you had no limitations. In Dr. Benjamin Hardy's incredible book, *The Science of Scaling,* he talks about having an impossible goal and attaching it to an impossible deadline. What if your big ambition was ten times what you are experiencing or producing today? What if you had three years to do it? You can't just run faster and work harder doing what you've always done. You have to let go of a lot of things that got you where you are and find new paths and people that will get you where you want to go. That's why starting with where you would like to be is so important.

Don't try to make this perfect because it won't be. It's just a first draft. As we go through the other elements of being a Beautiful Savage, we will come back to this and refine it.

Chapter 3

Normalizing New

Your net worth grows to the extent that you do.

—Ed Mylett

The key to reaching your big ambition is what I call "normalizing new." We all have a normal—a way we are currently navigating life in all the big areas we care about: relational, financial, physical, professional, and spiritual. If you were to follow someone around and observe how they're doing life, you could figure out what their normal is.

The normal is efficient. We do it on autopilot, relying on our subconscious mind while our conscious awareness takes a backseat. Repetition of your normal has already carved synaptic pathways that support our habitual way of living.

New is a different way of living your life in the future. The challenge is that it requires the conscious mind to take something new and normalize it—to move it from the conscious to the subconscious. That requires a different kind of energy and work. Generally, we're clumsy at it when we start. But as Randy said in the fable, this is where growth lives. We have to work to create the synaptic connections to make it muscle memory or a part of our normal.

"Normalizing new" explains why change is so difficult and why most people plateau. It's not just about having good intentions or even good plans—it's about understanding the neurological and habitual work required to make new behaviors automatic. This framework gives people a realistic understanding of why growth requires conscious effort and provides a pathway for making that effort systematic rather than random.

When you have a bigger ambition that is different from what you're currently experiencing, it requires you to begin to master some of the new. As the executive leadership coach Marshall Goldsmith said, "What got you here will not get you there."

The gravitational pull of all people and organizations is to defend the way we've always done things. Our greatest opportunity to recognize our future possibilities is not about abandoning our normal, nor is it about rejecting the new. It's about dancing with the tension between the two.

Reaching your big ambitions calls you to choose the new even in the wake of uncertainty. It requires you to prioritize tasks that are new even when you are busy with the normal.

Personal Example: Living the Framework

When I moved from Lubbock to Austin, I had no network of friends or family in Austin, but I wanted to do more meaningful and rewarding work. So, I took a job with a third-generation family-owned electrical contracting company. I met Jamie, who would become my wife and the mother of our two kids, Gage and Abby. I also created a network of people who had bigger ambitions, and one of those people led me to the financial services industry.

I walked away from the familiar electrical contracting role where I was making good money to go into commission-based financial services. We began going to Shoreline Church and understanding God had so much to say about living an extraordinary life, and we began to discover and apply those principles.

It certainly was not easy. We sold our house and moved to a small apartment to save money and to be closer to the training office. I sold the truck I loved for a more fuel-efficient car. When I wasn't meeting or trying to get meetings with clients, my nights and weekends were busy studying processes, products, business administration, human behavior, psychology, and practicing language. I faced daily setbacks and rejection. Our income had more drama than a French bulldog at bath time. And then there were the voices.

First the Accuser. *Listen to me carefully because I'm the only one telling you the truth here. You're not enough. You've never been enough, and deep down, you know it. All those people who say they believe in you? They're just being polite. They don't see what I see.*

You don't have what it takes. Look around—everyone else seems to have figured it out, but not you. You're stumbling through life pretending you know what you're doing, but we both know better.

You're going to let everyone down. Your family, your friends, the people counting on you—they're all going to realize they made a mistake putting their faith in you. And when they do, they'll leave. Of course they'll leave. Why would anyone stick around for this mess?

Honestly, it would have been better if they'd never met you in the first place. Think about how much easier their lives would be without your problems, your needs, your constant disappointments.

You should just quit now before you embarrass yourself further. You're never going to make it anyway. All this effort, all this trying—it's pointless. You're just delaying the inevitable.

Face it: You're all alone in this. Even surrounded by people, you're alone because nobody really understands the failure you are inside.

And that money situation? You should be afraid. Very afraid. It's all going to run out, and then what? Then everyone will see exactly what you're worth.

I'm the voice that keeps you grounded in reality. Everything else is just wishful thinking.

Have you heard this voice before? Isn't this voice a jerk? But there was a second voice too.

The voice of truth. *Stop. Listen to me instead. I am the voice that calls out above the storm of lies you've been hearing.*

You are enough—not because of what you do or accomplish, but because of who you are. Your worth isn't determined by your performance or other people's opinions. It's inherent, unchangeable, and real.

When the accuser whispers that you'll never make it, I remind you: you don't have to see the whole staircase to take the first step. Every giant was once a beginner. Every expert was once a disaster.

Those people in your life? They're not going anywhere because of your struggles. Real love doesn't flee at the first sign of imperfection—it shows up stronger. You are not a burden; you are beloved.

The fear of running out of money, of being alone, of failing—these are just shadows. They feel massive because you're looking at them instead of looking ahead to where you're going.

Like the song says, the voice of truth tells you a different story. It speaks of hope when despair tries to drown you out. It reminds you that you're not defined by your circumstances but by something far greater.

I am the voice that says: You are loved, you are capable, you belong here. The storm may be loud, but I am louder. The waves may be high, but you will not be swept away.

Listen for me above the noise. I am the voice of truth, and I will never stop calling your name.

I love this voice, and if you are going to do extraordinary things, be careful to listen to it when the accuser is whispering in your ear because that jerk likes to talk. There is a great song called "Voice of Truth" by Casting Crowns that was referred to above, and I would recommend you keep it on your daily playlist.

So in the face of all the struggle and difficulty, we began to build an extraordinary company. We began giving 10 percent of our income, which felt like an obstacle to many of the goals that we had, but it was actually an accelerator. When you start giving money to God, you begin to read the word of God in a very different way. "For where your treasure is, there your heart will be also" (Matthew 6:21, NIV).

Every time we brought on another team member, it was a step of faith. Every time we implemented new practices into our business that had not yet been a part of what had created our living and impact, it was a step of faith.

Today, we have an organization of over twenty people across the country that makes millions of dollars a year. At the time I'm writing this, we are in the middle of buying into our third multimillion-dollar financial planning partnership, and we are integrating systems and processes and thinking into that practice with the aspiration of massively increasing profitability and quality of life for all those involved.

These aren't abstract concepts—they're lived experiences that demonstrate how the "normalizing new" framework plays out in real decisions. Each example required choosing the uncertain future over the comfortable present. The tithing example is particularly powerful because it shows how spiritual principles can be practical accelerators, not just moral obligations.

The Parable of Normalizing New

In the fable, Randy relates the story Jesus told that perfectly illustrates the Beautiful Savage approach to growth. A master gave three servants different amounts of money (talents) before leaving on a journey. Two servants took risks, invested their talents, and doubled their money. The third servant played it safe, buried his talent, and returned only what he was given. If you read that section, then you know that the master celebrated the two who had taken risks, who had normalized new. He rewarded them with more responsibility and opportunities. The servant who defended his normal approach was condemned for it.

The gravitational pull is always toward your normal, toward burying your talents. It's safer. It's predictable. You can't lose what you were given. But Jesus is clear: Playing it safe with what you've been entrusted with isn't faithfulness—it's faithlessness.

Your talents—your abilities, your opportunities, your resources— they're not given to you to maintain. They're given to you to multiply. And multiplication requires normalizing new.

It is critical to have regular points throughout your year—quarterly at least—where you stop and think about where you want to be if you're living a rich life three years from today in all the areas that you care about: relational, financial, physical, professional, and spiritual.

Then you have to decide what kind of person you would need to become and what things you would need to do in order to move in that direction, as well as deciding what things are no longer serving you to get to that life.

Before moving forward, identify one thing you're currently doing that's "normal" but isn't serving your three-year vision. What's one new skill, habit, or approach that would move you closer to where you want to be relationally, professionally, financially, physically, and spiritually? Write both down—we'll use these in Chapter 5.

Chapter 4

The Energy Allocation Model

The successful warrior is the average man with laser-like focus.
—Bruce Lee

Why do so many successful people and companies plateau? It is not a lack of ideas or motivation—it's energy allocation.

You only have so much time and energy. You'll run out of energy way before you run out of ideas and tasks to do. If you use it all for normal, you have no energy for the new. It's a trap. If you don't have a lifestyle where you are regularly changing where you put your energy relative to normal, you will stagnate and eventually decline.

Think about a startup. When I came into the business, 75 percent of my energy was on new things, and 25 percent was on normal. The majority of my energy was spent learning things and figuring out what worked, which is inherently slow. You're problem-solving in real time.

But then you normalize some of that, you translate what you learned into repeatable systems, and you move to a 50-50 energy split.

Then at scale, when you have enough systems in place that 75 percent of your energy is focused on execution and optimization, the remaining 25 percent can go to innovation and further growth.

The challenge is that if you don't go back to 50 percent normal, 50 percent new (or sometimes 25 percent normal, 75 percent new), you will begin to plateau and eventually stagnate, because you can only run so fast and work so hard in your normal. To grow again, you have to do new things you haven't done and, in most cases, abandon some of your old thinking and methods.

The 75/25 → 50/50 → 25/75 → back to 50/50 cycle provides a framework for understanding the rhythm of sustainable growth. Most people understand the need to "work on the business, not just in the business," but this model quantifies it and makes it actionable.

The Talents Teach Energy Allocation

The parable of the talents that Randy spoke about in the fable reveals the secret of energy allocation. The two faithful servants didn't just work harder with what they had—they allocated their energy differently. They advanced from their normal (safe storage) and took a risk with new (investment).

The master's response was "To those who have, more will be given." As Randy said, it isn't about favoritism. It is the cumulative impact of consistently choosing growth over safety, new over normal.

The third servant stayed stuck in normal. He preserved rather than multiplied. He was busy but not productive; active but not growing. The master said, "Take the bag of gold from him and give it to the one who has ten bags." This servant's fate is a warning: When you refuse to allocate energy toward new possibilities, you don't just stay the same— you eventually lose what you had.

Jesus is teaching us that faithful stewardship requires the courage to risk what you have in order to gain what you could have. This is the essence of the energy allocation model—constantly cycling between the security of proven systems and the risk of unproven opportunities.

Your muscles follow the same principle Jesus outlined in the talents. When you allocate 100 percent of your energy to comfort (staying in your current strength), your muscles atrophy. When you allocate energy to new challenges (progressive overload), they grow.

The person who refuses to risk their current comfort level for new growth doesn't just stay the same—they actually get weaker. "To those who have [and use], more will be given." The compound effect of consistently choosing growth over safety creates exponential strength.

Every professional faces the talents dilemma: allocate energy toward mastering what you already know (safe) or developing new capabilities (risky). Those who bury their skills in the security of proven competence eventually find their expertise obsolete. Those who risk their current expertise to gain new skills multiply their value. The energy allocation model Jesus taught isn't just spiritual—it's career survival.

This is why the energy allocation model isn't optional for Beautiful Savages—it's stewardship in action.

The visual representation that follows shows why the energy allocation model is so critical—without intentionally returning to innovation phases, even successful businesses and entrepreneurs will plateau and eventually decline.

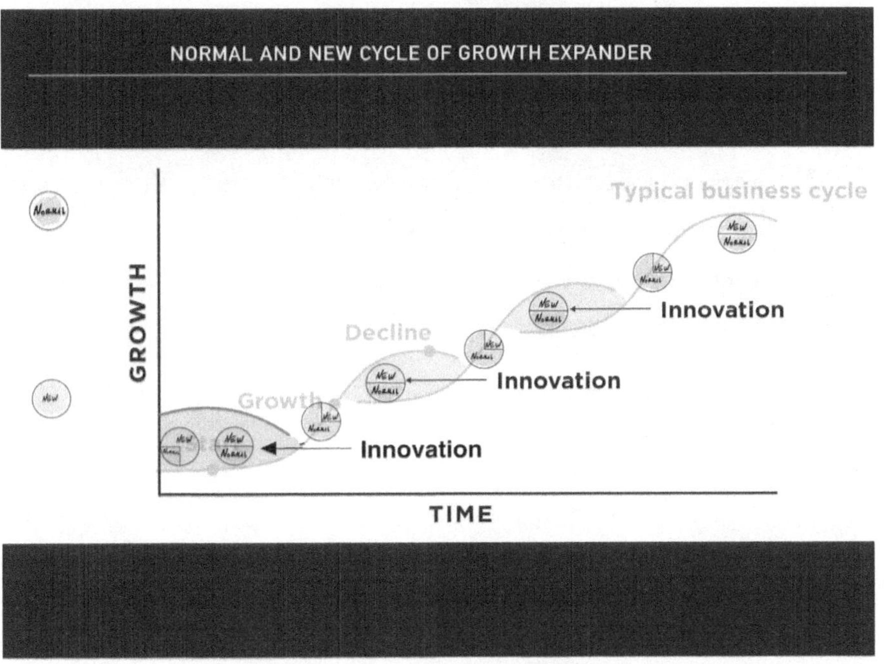

Figure 1B. Normal and New Cycle of Growth.

Key Insights from the Growth Cycle:

• **Growth Phase**: Heavy focus on new activities and innovation

• **Plateau Risk**: When you become too comfortable with "normal" operations

• **Innovation Points**: Strategic moments to introduce new systems, processes, or approaches

• **Sustained Growth**: Achieved through consistent cycling between normal efficiency and innovation

Consider the question that Randy asked Wes in the fable: "How much energy do you spend on what you already know versus learning something new?"

This week, pay attention to your energy allocation: What percentage of your time goes to "normal" versus "new"?

Just observe or note your tendencies for now. In the next chapter, we'll turn this awareness into action.

Chapter 5

The Activity Matrix Process

Until we can manage time, we can manage nothing else.
—Peter Drucker

One way to manage energy allocation is to do an activity matrix. Start by writing out the current activities you and your team are engaging in throughout your process on a regular basis. Now look at your big ambition—where do you want to go in the next three years? Then back that down into a one-year reverse-engineered version of those three years. Back it down again to 90 days, by asking what are good 90-day milestones to hit?

Then comes the key part. Of all the things that you could do that are new, what would move the needle the most in your opinion? What "normal" activities are your team currently doing that need to be abandoned or delegated to technology, an existing person on the team, or a new person?

The benefit of this is you can't do everything, but you can do a few things that will move the needle the most in a 90-day period. This creates urgency. The inspiration is the deadline. Then you put it on the calendar. When will you do these things to take them from new to normal?

This turns your big ambition from overwhelming to actionable through forced prioritization. The 3-year to 1-year to 90-day breakdown prevents analysis paralysis, while the activity matrix forces hard choices about what to stop doing. "Inspiration is the deadline" is a game-changing insight—without urgency, good intentions drift into someday/maybe territory. And the calendar component is crucial because it bridges the gap between intention and execution.

Don't Let Perfect Be the Enemy of Progress

Does all this feel overwhelming?

At this point, you might be tempted to keep rolling through the book without actually doing this exercise. You're thinking: "How do I know what I want in three years? How would I back it down to one year, then 90-days? Then I have to pick what I'm going to do about it?"

Let me give you a helpful tip that has worked for me and thousands of others I know: **Use AI as your thinking partner.**

Copy this exercise and put it into Claude.ai or ChatGPT and ask it to help by interviewing you—asking questions and walking you through this process step by step. In fact, that's not a bad idea for any of the exercises in this book.

Here's another pro tip: Don't type your answers into the response boxes in these tools. Simply speak them using the microphone button on either app. You'll be surprised at the speed and quality of output that results from this method.

Another suggestion is that if this is your first time going through this exercise, start with one of the big five areas; don't try to tackle them all at once. Since you are an entrepreneur, perhaps the professional realm is where you start. Taking a small bite by working all the way through the exercise in one area is better than not starting at all because you are waiting until you can fully capture everything. This is what I do when I am teaching our Transform Community for financial advisors that want to do meaningful holistic work (to learn about this, go to wesyounglive.com). I teach the big ambition exercise and have students spend fifteen minutes writing out what an extraordinary life would look like for them three years from today as best they can. Next, I have them focus only on their professional life. Since they are running financial planning businesses, I give them a template to fill in and modify (see the sample Peak Performance Path Template in the Resources section). This is specific to their industry, and many of the drivers and items on the to-do list come out of the eleven-session class we teach, but it should serve as a good reference for what I am describing. They walk away with a plan in at least one area.

It doesn't need to be perfect—I can promise you it won't be. But it won't be perfect if you keep putting it off either. In fact, delaying will just make your life less fulfilling.

Remember Randy's wisdom to Wes: "The gravitational pull is always toward burying your talents." Taking imperfect action beats perfect planning that never happens.

So before you turn the page, make a decision: Will you do a rough draft of this exercise in the next forty-eight hours, or will you let this become another good idea you never implement?

Grateful Condition— Cultivating Enjoyment

Chapter 6

The Strategic Power of Gratitude

Gratitude is not only the greatest of virtues but the parent of all others.
—Cicero

A grateful condition isn't passive appreciation. It's an active, strategic practice that serves three specific functions for Beautiful Savages:

1. **Evidence building:** It creates a documented track record of your capacity for growth. When you regularly catalog your greatest moments, you're building evidence that you can handle the next big challenge.

2. **Energy generation:** Unlike gratitude that makes you content with the status quo, a grateful condition generates energy for bigger ambitions. It's gratitude that says, "Look how far I've come" rather than "I should be satisfied with this."

3. **Confidence catalyst:** It transforms past victories into future courage. Your grateful condition becomes proof of concept for your next impossible thing.

As Randy said in the fable, a grateful condition is fuel. Strategic fuel. We can be so focused on where we want to go that we don't enjoy where we are, on our way to where we're going. And while exercising our big ambition, we will be going somewhere for the rest of our lives.

This reframes gratitude from a nice-to-have virtue into a performance enhancement tool. The insight that "we can be so focused on where we want to go that we don't enjoy where we are" captures a trap that driven people fall into constantly. Driven people fall into this trap because their wiring makes them natural gap-identifiers. They're constantly scanning for what's missing, what's broken, what needs improvement. This serves them well in business—it's how they spot opportunities and solve problems. But it becomes a liability when applied to their own lives.

Their dopamine system is calibrated for achievement, not appreciation. They get a hit from closing the gap, but that satisfaction is fleeting. Almost immediately, they identify the next gap, the next mountain to climb. It's like being addicted to the chase but allergic to the catch.

Without a grateful condition, driven people risk what I call "success depression"—the hollow feeling that comes when you realize achieving your goals didn't deliver the lasting satisfaction you expected. They build impressive businesses and bank accounts while remaining emotionally bankrupt.

More practically, they risk burnout, strained relationships, and ironically, decreased performance. When you never pause to acknowledge progress, you lose the very fuel that makes ambitious pursuits sustainable. Your team sees a leader who's never satisfied, your family feels like they're never enough, and you start making decisions from scarcity instead of abundance.

The ultimate risk is becoming successful but not significant—achieving everything on your list while missing the joy that makes the journey worthwhile. But this framework avoids the false choice between being grateful and being ambitious by positioning gratitude as fuel for ambition rather than a substitute for it.

Regular gratitude says, "I'm thankful for what I have."

Grateful condition says, "I'm amazed by what I've overcome, which gives me confidence for what I'll conquer next."

Rather than just "counting blessings," Beautiful Savages use grateful condition to:

- Review quarterly: "What did I accomplish that I once thought was impossible?"
- Extract patterns: "What conditions allowed me to succeed before?"
- Build momentum: "If I could do X, what else am I capable of?"

This powerful Beautiful Savage practice helps accelerate your capacity to get to your big ambition.

The Enjoyment Macronutrient Connection

This is where Arthur Brooks's research becomes profound for entrepreneurs. Enjoyment—one of the three macronutrients of happiness—is about pleasure combined with people combined with memories.

If you were to go back and look at the last ten years of your life—all the things you accomplished, experiences you had, incredible moments whether in work, relationships, or on vacation—I guarantee you one common denominator will emerge: enjoyment will come out of it, because it will involve memories that involve people that involve pleasure.

Pull out your phone and look at your pictures, because it'll stimulate some thinking around this. Notice that it wasn't always pleasurable during that time, but it was pleasurable after the outcome was achieved because you had to suffer or struggle through hard things.

Right now, name three things about your current business or life situation that you're genuinely grateful for. Write them down. Notice how this shifts your energy about pursuing your big ambition.

Chapter 7

The Greatest Moments Audit

The past is a source of knowledge, and the future is a source of hope.
—Stephen Ambrose

Let's take the three things you are grateful for that you noted in the last chapter and build those into a grateful condition. One exercise that I love is to do an audit of your greatest moments. Take a time period like ten years in the past and write out all your greatest moments—the things you're most proud of, the highlight reel experiences that you've had, things you've accomplished. Note your age ten years ago and your age now, but also the ages of your kids, your spouse, the people that were part of your team ten years ago and today.

Seeing the difference between where you were and where you are now will do two things. One, it will give you an amazing sense of gratitude over how far you've come. Second, it will give you a surprising amount of confidence in what you are capable of and actually fuel the energy you need for the next big jump.

This practice serves as both a gratitude builder and a confidence builder. By looking at where everyone was ten years ago versus now, you're creating evidence of your capacity to create positive change.

If you want to deep dive on the greatest moments list, check out *All It Takes Is a Goal* by Jon Acuff. In my opinion, every entrepreneur should read it. Acuff discusses how reflecting on and writing down past successes, both big and small, makes them concrete and easy to revisit when you need motivation or confidence to overcome the next challenge.

Another great exercise I mentioned briefly in the last chapter is to go back through your phone and look at your pictures. We all have thousands of photos that represent moments we chose to capture—that's data. It will bring back many great memories, but it will also highlight the things you value and that bring you joy.

When you do this exercise, pay attention to these things: How are you wired? What do you like? What is a rich life to you?

Use your findings to inform where you want to go from here and tweak your big ambition.

A great tool that facilitates this exercise is the Mind Expander Worksheet found in the Resources section. Part one of the Mind Expander gives you a template to write out your greatest moments list over the last decade in all the big areas of life. It also has a place to write the date and ages of you and your family ten years ago (that will show you how fast time goes). Part two gives you a template to write out the greatest moments and accomplishments you hope to experience over the next decade in all the big areas of your life. It also has a place to write the date and ages of you and your family ten years from now. Part three allows you to list your top three from each of the first two sections. Yes, I know this is hard, but boy is it necessary. In the last part, you funnel everything down to four one-year goals.

Every 90 days when I do this exercise, I am amazed at what takes place in my mind, body, and spirit. It builds an amazing sense of gratitude for the present and gives me an incredible amount of confidence and awe about what is possible for the future. I always find it powerful to do this before I update my big ambition on my 3-year, 1-year, 90-day plans.

Take the time now to start your greatest moments audit using the Mind Expander Worksheet. Then, use the output of that audit to go back to your big ambition exercise (Chapter 2) and refine it. I have found that having this as a foundation really helps to expand my ambition in both impact and enjoyment.

Let this grateful condition be the fuel that helps you reach your goals.

Chapter 8

The 90-Day Gratitude Rhythm

Gratitude makes sense of our past, brings peace for today,
and creates a vision for tomorrow.

—Melody Beattie

One greatest moments audit won't transform your life. Just like one workout won't make you fit, one business plan won't make you successful, and one date won't build a marriage. The power of the grateful condition isn't in the single event—it's in the rhythm.

Most people treat gratitude like a New Year's resolution: They do it once with great intention, feel inspired for a few days, then drift back into the relentless pursuit of what's next. But Beautiful Savages understand that grateful condition requires the same systematic approach as any other business discipline. You wouldn't run your finances, team meetings, or client relationships on a "when I feel like it" mentality. Your grateful condition deserves the same consistency.

The 90-day rhythm creates a cadence that keeps you calibrated—grateful enough to enjoy the journey, confident enough to take the next leap. Without this rhythm, you'll either stagnate in comfortable appreciation or burn out chasing the next milestone. With it, you stay in the sweet spot where contentment fuels ambition instead of competing with it.

Every 90 days you should update your grateful condition list by going through that same exercise I discussed in the previous chapter. You will also revisit your big ambition every 90 days, backing the 3-year down to a 1-year down to a 90-day plan.

This creates the complete rhythm where every 90 days you're feeding both sides of the Beautiful Savage equation:

- **Big Ambition**: Where am I going next? (3-year → 1-year → 90-day planning)
- **Grateful Condition**: Where have I been? (Greatest moments audit, progress tracking)

This prevents both stagnation (from not pushing forward) and ingratitude (from not acknowledging progress). It's a systematic way to consistently reach your goals without burning out. Over time, this creates a rich archive of growth and achievements.

Now you have your fuel. Your big ambition gives you direction and meaning. Your grateful condition gives you confidence and energy. But between where you are today and where you want to be stands the thing that stops most people cold: resistance.

You've mapped where you're going and celebrated how far you've come. The gap between these two points isn't going to close itself. It requires action—consistent, persistent, sometimes uncomfortable, action. And that's exactly where most well-intentioned plans die.

The difference between dreamers and achievers isn't better planning or stronger motivation. It's the willingness to dance with the resistance that lives in that gap. Let's talk about how to do that.

Savage Persistence—
Earning Satisfaction Through Resistance

Chapter 9

The Beauty of Earned Success

Success is not final, failure is not fatal: it is the
courage to continue that counts.

—Winston Churchill

In the book *Atomic Habits*, James Clear talks about the difference between motion and action. Motion is when you're preparing to do things —which in large part is what we've been discussing: creating a big ambition, marinating on your grateful condition, and going through the exercises.

Action is when we begin to live. You begin to do the things on your 90-day action plan that you believe are going to move you in the direction of that big ambition.

This addresses the gap between knowing and doing that derails so many well-intentioned people. The *Atomic Habits* motion vs. action framework perfectly captures why planning can become a substitute for progress rather than a catalyst for it. Planning gives the feeling of action without the risk of failure. But it is savage persistence that bridges the gap between good intentions and actual results.

Savage persistence—to dance with the resistance between where you are and where you want to be—is the key. Many people have great plans and actually have a grateful heart, but it is their actions that will determine their outcomes.

The Satisfaction Macronutrient Connection

Have you ever had a well-intentioned plan that you didn't implement because it was difficult or there never seemed to be time? Of course you do, we all do, and it doesn't feel good. Because as Arthur Brooks discovered, **you can't have satisfaction without overcoming hard things.** Think back to your greatest moments audit. If you're like most people, the sweetest victories came only after you endured challenges, setbacks, and a little pain along the way. Like Ed Mylett said, "You can't have a million-dollar dream with a minimum-wage work ethic."

I like to equate it to going to the gym in the morning. I don't wake up thrilled to sweat and suffer through a bunch of reps or a couple of miles. It's hard, sometimes it hurts. But pushing through and accomplishing that thing is what makes it satisfying. I chose to take action toward better health. Life works the same way.

This is why the gap between where you are and where you want to be is where satisfaction lives. When you choose not to trade what you want ultimately for what you can have immediately, you create the conditions for deep satisfaction. You work toward what you want, and you enjoy the process along the way.

Let's start taking action. Look at your big ambition from Chapter 2. What's the first concrete action you could take this week to move from motion to action? Put it on your calendar now.

Chapter 10

Understanding Resistance

The cave you fear to enter holds the treasure you seek.

—Joseph Campbell

Resistance is the invisible force that stands between where you are today and where you want to be. This force shows up in three primary forms:

1. Fear
2. Fatigue
3. Arrogance

We all know it's easier to be on autopilot—to do things the way you've always done them—than to face these monsters. But where is the satisfaction in that?

Beautiful Savages know resistance isn't bad. It's a requirement for recognizing your greatness.

And savage persistence is the key to dancing with that resistance.

Positioning resistance as the pathway to greatness, instead of seeing it as the enemy, is profound because it changes how you relate to obstacles. They become confirmation you're on the right path rather than evidence you should quit. The metaphor of dancing with the resistance suggests grace and partnership rather than brute-force grinding.

Let's look at each of these forms of resistance and how you can dance with them.

Chapter 11

Fear—Face Everything and Rise

Courage is not the absence of fear, but action in spite of it.
—Mark Twain

You must dance with fear. There is a difference between experiencing emotional fear and being afraid—dancing with the emotion of fear versus being afraid.

Two great acronyms for the word fear: **Face Everything and Run** or **Face Everything and Rise.**

A Beautiful Savage faces everything and rises.

I love what Jesus taught about this. He was constantly telling his disciples, "Don't be afraid." He told them that because he was continually putting them in environments where they were going to experience the emotion of fear. The difference is, you can experience fear but not take on the identity of being afraid.

Courage is not the absence of fear. It is an identity you take on when the emotion of fear shows up. You face everything you're afraid of, and you rise.

People who say they're not afraid, and maybe even act optimistic, are ungrounded optimists. They don't think through all the possibilities that could and should create the emotion of fear, and face them.

Beautiful Savages dance with the fear and rise.

Why is this better than ungrounded optimism? Because when you acknowledge fear and rise anyway, you build genuine confidence. Ungrounded optimists avoid looking at potential problems, which leaves them unprepared when reality hits. They're like someone walking into a boxing match saying, "I'm not worried about getting punched," instead of training to handle the punches they know are coming.

When you face everything and rise, you develop what psychologists call "earned confidence"—the deep assurance that comes from having stared down real challenges and overcome them. You're not pretending obstacles don't exist; you're proving you can handle them when they do.

Ungrounded optimists crumble at the first sign of real resistance because their confidence was built on denial, not experience. Beautiful Savages grow stronger with each challenge because their confidence is built on evidence—evidence that they can feel afraid and act anyway.

This approach also builds trust with others. People can sense the difference between someone who's naive about challenges and someone who sees them clearly but moves forward regardless. One inspires false confidence; the other inspires genuine followership.

Think of it like taking a trip with your crazy uncle. You let him come on the trip, but you don't let him drive.

This framework distinguishes between the emotion of fear (which is information) and the identity of being afraid (which is limitation). The "crazy uncle" analogy works because it suggests you can acknowledge fear without being controlled by it.

What specifically are you afraid of about pursuing your big ambition? Name it.

Chapter 12

Fatigue—The Energy Thief

Fatigue makes cowards of us all.

—Jimmy Johnson

Savage persistence to dance with the resistance also requires you to physically schedule activities that will help you normalize the new ideas, activities, values, and thought processes into your week to avoid fatigue.

When it comes to normalizing new, it's not about how long it will take. It's about how many observed iterations it will take to move it from the conscious mind to the subconscious, to create the synaptic connections to make it a part of the normal. You also want to iterate on it and make it better.

This requires time every week to evaluate the new things that you're trying to blend into the normal. How did it go? What could you have done better? What do you need to work on?

Change is like remodeling a house while you're trying to live in it. It is messy, it's inconvenient, and it's actually less effective initially than if you would've just left everything alone. You can already fill up your day with normal activities and still not get to everything on your normal list. New ideas require more energy, and they require you to do less normal. New ideas are clunky—you're not good at them yet. They are not muscle memory.

I remember being with my friend Michael Broderick at a conference that we go to every year. We got to the conference room before the main speakers came on stage, and we started comparing notes from the previous year's conference. We had a bunch of stuff circled, a bunch of stuff starred, some of it highlighted, and some had all three. Many of the ideas each of us had captured were the same. These were ideas that we thought were going to lead us to our next big jump.

Then we discussed how many of them we did. Do you know how many? Zero.

We were not afraid to do them, but fatigue makes cowards of us all. The gravitational pull of all people and organizations is to defend or even subconsciously drift back into the normal—the way they've always done it.

The house remodeling analogy perfectly captures why change feels so difficult even when we want it. The Michael Broderick story is devastating in its honesty—two successful people with the same great ideas implementing zero of them. "Fatigue makes cowards of us all" explains why good intentions aren't enough.

What "normal" activities are draining energy from your "new" goals? List three. Where on your calendar can you block out time for new at the beginning of your daily routine? Maybe listening to a podcast on your drive to the gym or office. Protected time to practice or implement a new project each week? Now do it! Put it on the calendar.

Chapter 13

Arrogance—Success-Induced Blindness

The greatest enemy of knowledge is not ignorance,
it is the illusion of knowledge.

—Stephen Hawking

Arrogance is an attitude of superiority and self-importance that manifests as treating others with condescension or dismissiveness. Ironically, success can lead to arrogance.

When you believe your way is the best way and you can point to your current results, it can accelerate your arrogance and blind you to seeing and seeking out things that are going to get you to your next big jump.

You'll say things like "I'm doing pretty well the way I'm doing it. Look at all the success I've had."

It reminds me of the Blockbuster Video/Netflix story. My father was an operations director for a large franchise of Blockbuster Video. In the year 2000, I remember him telling me he felt like their days were numbered in the business. Keep in mind, in 2000 Blockbuster was a $6 billion giant. They dominated the home entertainment space through their almost ten thousand retail video rental stores.

The founders of Netflix met with the Blockbuster Video board of directors and pitched that Blockbuster should buy them for $50 million. They could be their online mail-delivery video rental arm. Blockbuster flatly declined.

At the time, the founders of Netflix would say it was the worst day of their lives, but later the best. They could never have become what they were capable of if Blockbuster had actually bought them, because they were too stuck in the normal.

Ten years later, Blockbuster had filed for bankruptcy and Netflix was over a $9 billion company. As I write this, Netflix is a $552 billion behemoth that dominates the home entertainment space. They have reinvented themselves over and over again, constantly normalizing new into the rhythm of their operation. It's not that everything they've tried has worked, but enough worked to make them who they are today.

Arrogance is perhaps the most subtle and dangerous form of resistance because it masquerades as wisdom. The Blockbuster story is the perfect illustration because it wasn't a struggling company making this mistake—it was a dominant market leader. Success can create blind spots that prevent the very innovation needed for continued success.

Where might you be too attached to "how you've always done it"? What feedback have you been dismissing?

Chapter 14

Dancing with Resistance—The Antidotes

The master has failed more times than the beginner has even tried.
—Stephen McCranie

We know now how important resistance is to our growth, and we know that feeling it tells us we're on the right track. But how do we have the savage persistence to dance with it?

Each form of resistance has a specific antidote. These antidotes take work, but remember that work is where the satisfaction lives. As Randy told Wes in the fable, "On the other side of that resistance lives the most beautiful, savage version of yourself."

For Fear → You Need Faith
Face Everything and Rise

Fear whispers: "You're not ready. You don't have enough experience. What if you fail?"

Faith responds: "I don't need to see the whole staircase to take the first step."

Fear tempts us to trade our ultimate goal for immediate comfort. But faith keeps us tracking toward our big ambition. You have to remember why you're doing what you set out to do—and that the impact of dancing with fear will be greater than staying in your normal.

This faith is rooted in your grateful condition. Remember what you've overcome, the great moments you've had, the obstacles you've already conquered. You've already done so much. Use this as evidence that you are more than capable of tackling what's next.

Look back at your greatest moments audit. I guarantee many of those victories came after you felt afraid but acted anyway. You once prayed for many of the things you have right now. And you can do it again.

Practical faith in action:
- When fear whispers, "What if I fail?"; faith responds, "What if I succeed beyond my wildest dreams?"
- When fear says, "I'm not qualified," faith says, "I'll become qualified by doing the work."
- When fear asks, "What will people think?"; faith asks, "What will I think of myself if I don't try?"

Randy's Wisdom: Remember what Randy taught Wes—you can let fear come on the trip, but you don't let it drive. Acknowledge the emotion, then choose the identity of someone who faces everything and rises.

For Fatigue → You Need Systematic Action
Schedule the New First

Fatigue is the most insidious form of resistance because it feels so reasonable. "I'm too busy with current clients to pursue new markets. I'm too tired to learn new systems. I'll do it when things calm down."

But here's the truth: Things never calm down. The gravitational pull toward normal is relentless.

The conference story reveals the real problem: Michael Broderick and I had the same brilliant ideas, circled and starred with enthusiasm. But we implemented zero of them. Not because we were afraid, but because fatigue made cowards of us.

Systematic action means:

1. **Scheduling the new activities first, when your energy is highest.** Don't hope you'll have energy left over—you won't. Tuesday mornings for trying new techniques. Thursday evenings for system development. Saturday early for strategic thinking.

2. **Applying the delegation decision tree.** Before adding anything new, ask:
   - Can this be eliminated completely?
   - Can this be automated with technology?
   - Can this be delegated to an existing team member?
   - Can this be delegated to a new hire?
   - Does this absolutely require my unique expertise?

3. **Measuring normalization progress.** How do you know when something has moved from "new" to "normal"? When you can do it without conscious thought, when it no longer drains unusual energy, when others can replicate it.

The entrepreneur's delegation dilemma: "No one can do it as well as I can." This is usually true—initially. But ask yourself: "Would I rather have something done at 80 percent of my quality while I focus on activities that only I can do, or would I rather stay stuck doing everything myself?"

Randy's Energy Allocation Wisdom: Remember how Randy scheduled different types of fishing for different energy levels. He didn't hope he'd have energy for trying new techniques—he scheduled them when his energy was naturally the highest.

For Arrogance → You Need Humility
Stay Curious, Stay Growing

Arrogance is the most dangerous form of resistance because it disguises itself as wisdom. "I've been successful doing it this way. Why would I change?"

Remember, Blockbuster asked that question. They were a $6 billion giant when Netflix offered to be their online arm for $50 million. Their success blinded them to the future.

Humility in practice means:

1. **Actively seeking feedback.** Schedule quarterly feedback sessions with team members, clients, and mentors, and ask: "What am I missing? Where are my blind spots? What should I be paying attention to that I'm not?"

2. **Assuming you don't know what you don't know.** Before making decisions, ask: "Who else has faced this challenge? What can I learn from their experience? What assumptions am I making?"

3. **Respecting expertise at every level.** The newest team member might see something you've become blind to. The client's complaint might reveal a market shift you've missed. Humility

creates an environment where new ideas can surface.

4. **Regularly questioning your methods.** Just because something worked doesn't mean it's still the best way. Ask: "If I were starting this business today, would I do this the same way?"

Randy's Humility Lesson: Remember when Randy struggled with his new fishing techniques, admitting he was "terrible at it right now"? His willingness to be bad at something new is what kept him growing when others plateaued.

The Integration Effect

Here's what happens when you apply these antidotes consistently:

Faith transforms fear into fuel. Instead of avoiding challenges, you start seeking them because you know they lead to growth.

Systematic action transforms fatigue into momentum. Instead of exhaustion from reactive firefighting, you experience the energizing flow of proactive progress.

Humility transforms arrogance into wisdom. Instead of defending old methods, you become a learning machine, constantly evolving and improving.

Each antidote reinforces the others: Faith gives you courage to act systematically. Systematic action builds evidence that supports faith. Humility keeps you open to better systems and deeper faith.

Your Resistance Assessment

Right now, identify which form of resistance is strongest in your life:

If it's fear: What specific outcome are you afraid of? Write it down.

Now, write down three pieces of evidence from your grateful condition that prove you can handle whatever comes.

If it's fatigue: What "new" activity have you been meaning to implement for months? Put it on your calendar this week, during your highest energy time.

If it's arrogance: What feedback have you been dismissing? Who could you ask for an honest assessment of your blind spots?

Remember Randy's final words to Wes: "On the other side of that resistance lives the most beautiful, savage version of yourself—the version God always intended."

Resistance isn't your enemy. It's your invitation to greatness.

The Integrated Beautiful Savage Life

Chapter 15

The 90-Day Beautiful Savage Rhythm

We are what we repeatedly do. Excellence, then,
is not an act, but a habit.

—Aristotle

You've done the work. You've identified your sacred gap and crafted your big ambition. You've conducted your greatest moments audit and built your grateful condition. You've named your resistance and learned to dance with fear, fatigue, and arrogance through faith, systematic action, and humility.

But here's what separates Beautiful Savages from people who attend seminars, read books, and get temporarily inspired: **rhythm**.

The framework you now understand isn't a one-time transformation —it's a lifestyle. The gap between where you are and where you want to be will never disappear. It will just move to a higher level. And that's not a bug in the system—it's the feature that keeps you fully alive.

Living the Integrated System Daily

Your big ambition isn't a destination you reach and then coast. It's a compass that guides your daily decisions. When someone asks for your time, you filter it through your three-year vision. When opportunities arise, you ask: "Does this serve others while moving me further into my gap?"

Your grateful condition isn't a gratitude journal you keep sporadically. It's a lens through which you view setbacks and victories. When challenges arise, you remember what you've already overcome. When success comes, you celebrate it as evidence of your capacity for the next level.

Your savage persistence isn't occasional bursts of motivation. It's your default response to resistance. When fear whispers, you automatically respond with faith. When fatigue threatens, you lean on your systems. When arrogance creeps in, you seek feedback and stay curious.

The Quarterly Rhythm That Changes Everything

Here's how Beautiful Savages maintain this integration:

Every 90 days, complete this cycle:
1. **Update your big ambition.** *(Meaning Macronutrient)*
   - Review your 3-year vision: Is it still compelling? Does it still serve others?
   - Back it down to a 1-year plan: What must happen this year to put my 3-year vision within reach?
   - Create your 90-day milestones: What specific outcomes will prove progress?
2. **Refresh your grateful condition.** *(Enjoyment Macronutrient)*
   - Conduct your greatest moments audit for the past quarter.
   - Document evidence of growth, progress, and capacity.

° Build confidence for the challenges ahead.

3. **Assess your current resistance.** *(Satisfaction Macronutrient)*

   ° Which form is showing up most: fear, fatigue, or arrogance?

   ° Apply the appropriate antidote with specific actions.

   ° Schedule the "new" activities that will normalize over the next 90 days.

4. **Take systematic action.**

   ° Calendar your new activities first, during peak energy times.

   ° Delegate or delete activities that no longer serve your ambition.

   ° Create weekly iteration cycles to improve and normalize.

Why 90 Days?

It's **long enough** to see real progress and build meaningful momentum. But **short enough** to maintain urgency and prevent drift. It's **frequent enough** to course-correct before small problems become major obstacles. And **sustainable enough** to maintain for years without burnout.

This rhythm prevents the two failure modes that kill most ambitious plans:

1. **The planning trap**: Endlessly refining your vision without taking action.

2. **The execution trap**: Getting so busy with daily activities that you lose sight of the bigger picture.

Your Beautiful Savage Operating System

Think of this 90-day rhythm as your personal operating system—the background processes that keep everything running optimally:

Week 1-12: Execute your plan with systematic action.

Week 13: Pause, assess, and recalibrate for the next quarter.

During execution weeks, you're living in the framework. During assessment week, you're working on the framework. Revisit the Beautiful Savage Assessment you took in Chapter 1. Review your scores and compare them with where you began. Which areas have grown stronger? Where are you still facing resistance?

Use these insights to fuel your next 90-day rhythm and identify the practices that will most accelerate your transformation.

The compound effect over time is staggering. Four quarters of this rhythm means four cycles of growth, four grateful condition audits building your confidence, four resistance assessments keeping you sharp. After just one year, you'll have normalized activities that seemed impossible at the start.

The Integration Promise

When you live this rhythm consistently, something remarkable happens: **The three macronutrients of happiness become automatic.**

Your **meaning** comes from pursuing ambitions that serve others. Your **enjoyment** comes from regular celebration of progress and growth. Your **satisfaction** comes from consistently overcoming worthy resistance.

You stop living in fragments—achieving but not enjoying, being grateful but lacking ambition, being driven but not fulfilled. You become integrated.

Your Next 90 Days Start Now

Before you close this book, schedule your first quarterly review 90 days from today. Put it on your calendar as a nonnegotiable appointment with your future self.

Then ask yourself: *What would you attempt if you knew you couldn't fail? What would you build if you had unlimited resources and unlimited time?*

The gap between where you are and where you want to be isn't a problem to solve—it's a sacred space to inhabit. The resistance you'll face isn't an obstacle to overcome—it's an invitation to become the most beautiful, savage version of yourself.

**You have two lives: the life you live,
and the unlived life within you.**

This rhythm ensures they get closer together every 90 days.

Love the Battle, Live with Joy

This isn't about choosing between being driven OR being happy. It's about understanding that for entrepreneurs, the path to happiness runs directly through the battle.

You don't have to apologize for your ambition. You don't have to choose between success and joy. You don't have to defend your desire to build something better.

You are designed to want more, to build more, to become more. The gap between where you are and where you want to be isn't a character flaw—it's the source of your aliveness.

> *The glory of God is man fully alive,*
> *and the life of man is the vision of God.*
>
> —Saint Irenaeus

Most entrepreneurs live in fragments:
- They achieve but don't enjoy.
- They're grateful but lack ambition.
- They're driven but not fulfilled.

Beautiful Savages integrate all three macronutrients of happiness into the entrepreneurial journey.

Meaning through big ambitions that serve others. **Enjoyment** through grateful reflection on the journey. **Satisfaction** through persistent engagement with worthy resistance.

This is your permission slip to be fully yourself. To love the battle while living with joy. To embrace the paradox that makes you who you are.

You have two lives—the life you live, and the unlived life within you. Between those two stands resistance.

Dance with it. Rise through it. Love every minute of it.

Because on the other side of that resistance lives the most beautiful, savage version of yourself.

This is your invitation to become a Beautiful Savage:

Beautiful *in the way you love your people, your purpose, God.*

Savage *in the way you conquer fear, overcome resistance, and create value.*

Welcome to the battle. Welcome to the joy.

Resources

The Beautiful Savage Assessment

Purpose: This assessment helps you discover how strongly you embody the traits of a Beautiful Savage. It's not a judgment, but a baseline. Completing it now will help you see your starting point and track your growth.

Instructions:

1. Read each statement.
2. Rate yourself on a scale of 1–5:

    1 = Strongly Disagree,

    2 = Disagree,

    3 = Neutral,

    4 = Agree,

    5 = Strongly Agree.

3. Add up your scores for each section.
4. Reflect on your strengths and areas for growth.

Part 1: Big Ambition (Meaning)

1. I have a clear vision of where I want to be three years from now.

2. My goals serve not just myself, but also my family, faith, and community.

3. I regularly think about the gap between where I am and where I want to be.

4. I take steps to normalize new skills, habits, or opportunities that push me forward.

5. I can articulate a sense of purpose that gives meaning to my work.

Subtotal (out of 25): __________

Part 2: Grateful Condition (Enjoyment)

6. I regularly pause to reflect on what I've accomplished and enjoyed.

7. I actively practice gratitude for both small and large moments.

8. I keep track of my "greatest moments" so I can revisit them.

9. I balance ambition with appreciation for the present.

10. I share gratitude with others, celebrating progress as well as outcomes.

Subtotal (out of 25): __________

Part 3: Savage Persistence (Satisfaction)

11. I view resistance (fear, fatigue, arrogance) as an opportunity, not an enemy.

12. When I feel fear, I still take action in the direction of my ambition.

13. I schedule and protect time for new or difficult activities.

14. I ask for feedback and stay humble, even after success.

15. I push through discomfort because I know satisfaction lies on the other side.

Subtotal (out of 25): __________

Scoring and Reflection

61–75 → You are living as a Beautiful Savage. Keep refining and deepening your practice.

46–60 → You embody many traits but may lack consistency in one or two areas. Identify where to grow.

31–45 → You have good intentions but need systems and support to sustain them.

15–30 → You are at the beginning of this journey. Awareness is the first step. This book will guide you forward.

Reflection Questions:

- Which domain is strongest for me?
- Which domain is weakest, and what small action could strengthen it?
- What surprised me about my scores?

Peak Performance Path

3 Year Vision

When clients engage in our annual planning process, it increases their profitability and quality of life.

We generate _____________________ in annual consulting revenue, _________________ in monthly retainer fees and ____________ in project-based engagements. Our ____________ person team of peak performers operates as a full-service business consulting firm. We have _________ retainer clients and generate _______________ in recurring monthly revenue. I have a Project Manager who oversees all active engagements. They manage the scope, timeline, and deliverables from kickoff to completion. We do a Discovery Session with every new client, and all existing clients are on an annual cadence of Quarterly Business Reviews and Year-End Strategy Sessions. We average _______ new client referrals per month. We have a Client Success Coordinator who is excellent at driving new engagements to completion and handling all client communication without me needing to be involved. We have _____________ in liquid reserves.

1 Year Vision

When clients engage in our annual planning process, it increases their profitability and quality of life.

We generate _____________________ in annual consulting revenue, _________________ in monthly retainer fees and ____________ in project-based engagements. Our ____________ person team of peak performers operates as a full-service business consulting firm. We have

__________ retainer clients and generate _______________ in recurring monthly revenue. I have a Project Manager who oversees all active engagements. They manage the scope, timeline, and deliverables from kickoff to completion. We do a Discovery Session with every new client, and all existing clients are on an annual cadence of Quarterly Business Reviews and Year-End Strategy Sessions. We average _______ new client referrals per month. We have a Client Success Coordinator who is excellent at driving new engagements to completion and handling all client communication without me needing to be involved. We have _____________ in liquid reserves.

90 Day Milestones

When clients engage in our annual planning process, it increases their profitability and quality of life.

We generated ________________ in consulting revenue, ________________ in retainer fees and ______________ in project-based engagements.

- We had ________ Discovery Sessions with prospective clients and ________ Quarterly Business Reviews with existing retainer clients.
- We are using the Discovery Framework & Engagement Checklists to prepare for all of our client meetings.
- We are using the monthly client dashboard and engagement review for all clients we have engaged with through the above actions.
- We prescheduled ________ Quarterly Business Review sessions for Q2 by 1/15/25.
- We prescheduled ________ Year-End Strategy Sessions for Q3/Q4 by 1/15/25.
- We operate from a weekly team block calendar.
- We hired a Client Success Coordinator who is excellent at driving new engagements to completion and handling all client communication without me being involved.
- We hired a Project Manager who oversees all active engagements and follows the Discovery Framework and Engagement Checklists to prepare me for all of my client meetings. They manage scope, timeline, and deliverables using the monthly engagement review with every client.

• I have identified and completed ______ continuing education and certification requirements to earn my CMC (Certified Management Consultant).

• I have identified and completed requirements to be recognized as a thought leader in my area of specialization through speaking, publishing, or industry awards.

• I have mastered the operational efficiency and growth strategy frameworks on the Engagement Checklist to increase my ability to diagnose and solve complex business problems.

• I spend two hours per week studying industry trends, case studies, and continuing education content in my areas of specialization.

• I signed up for the next industry conference or advanced training in my area of consulting.

90 Day Action Plan (Put it on the Calendar)

When clients engage in our annual planning process, it increases their profitability and quality of life.

We generate _______________ in consulting revenue, _______________ in retainer fees and _______________ in project-based engagements.

- Identify _________ prospective clients to set up Discovery Sessions with using proven diagnostic framework.
- Use the Discovery Framework with all new prospective clients I meet with.
- Use the Discovery Framework & Engagement Checklists to prepare for all of our client meetings.
- Use the monthly client dashboard and engagement review for all clients we have engaged with through the above actions.
- Preschedule 2025 Quarterly Business Reviews (Q2) and Year-End Strategy Sessions (Q3 and Q4) by 1/15/25.
- We operate from a weekly team block calendar.
- Hire a Client Success Coordinator who is excellent at driving new engagements to completion and handling all client communication without me being involved.
- Hire a Project Manager who oversees all active engagements and follows the Discovery Framework and Engagement Checklists to prepare me for all of my client meetings. They manage scope, timeline, and deliverables using the monthly engagement review with every client.
- Identify and complete _________ continuing education and certification requirements to earn my CMC.

• Identify and complete requirements to be recognized as a thought leader in my area of specialization through speaking, publishing, or industry awards.

• Spend two hours per week studying industry trends, case studies, and continuing education content in my areas of specialization.

• Sign up for the next industry conference or advanced training in my area of consulting.

• Study the operational efficiency and growth strategy frameworks on the Engagement Checklist for 1 hour per week and listen to a business strategy podcast weekly.

Mind Expander

Grateful Condition	Exciting Vision
Decade Behind - Great Moments & Accomplishments (Professionally, Relationally, Financially, Physically, Spiritually)	Decade Ahead - Great Moments & Accomplishments (Professionally, Relationally, Financially, Physically, Spiritually)
Date: Ages:	Date: Ages:

Top Three:

1.
2.
3.

Top Three:

1.
2.
3.

One-Year Goals

1.	2.	3.	4.

Acknowledgments

To my wife, Jamie—you have been the unwavering champion of every big ambition I've dared to pursue. You found Shoreline Church and led me to discover the real original Beautiful Savage. My life has never been the same, and I have you to thank. You are my greatest blessing.

To Gage and Abby—watching you evolve into the wonderful people you are has taught me so much about legacy, purpose, love, tenacity, and adventure. I am proud of who you are. Continue to have a big ambition, a grateful condition, and a savage persistence to dance with the resistance between the life you're living and the unlived life within you.

To my mom and dad—you gave me something more valuable than any monetary inheritance. Dad, you have been my greatest inspiration and best friend my entire life—the closest thing to the embodiment of Jesus this side of eternity. To Jim and Phyllis—thank you for raising the woman who would become my partner in this journey, and for modeling how love multiplies when given freely.

To Randy Marshall—you never called yourself my mentor, but five years of wisdom says otherwise. The character in this book represents you and every Beautiful Savage who saw potential in me when I couldn't see it myself.

To those who made this book possible—Nicole Schuette, my Beautiful Savage editor; Cap Daniels, who guided me through publishing;

and Mike Scovel, whose foreword and friendship through my most challenging seasons kept me dancing with resistance instead of running from it.

To the Beautiful Savage team I get to be a part of—Stephanie, Cara, Preston, Justin, Cheryl, Daniel, Lori, Seth, Jordan, and Lauren—we've danced with a lot of resistance together. To Dev Warren, Barry Cox, and Dr. John Branch—your endorsements mean the world, but your friendships mean more. To the thought leaders whose work shaped this framework—Arthur Brooks, Steven Pressfield, Andy Stanley, and Andy Andrews—thank you for giving language to what I was experiencing.

And ultimately, to Jesus—the original Beautiful Savage—who showed us that the path to abundant life runs through the sacred gap between where we are and where God is calling us to be. The glory of God truly is man fully alive.

This book exists because of all of you.

About the Author

Wesley Young is an entrepreneur, financial strategist, and sought-after speaker who has dedicated his career to helping successful individuals and families unlock their full potential. As the founder of a nationwide financial planning organization with twenty team members across the country, Wesley has built a multimillion-dollar enterprise by applying the Beautiful Savage principles he shares in this book.

Wesley's journey from electrical contractor to successful entrepreneur began with a leap of faith in 2003 when he transitioned into the financial services industry. Through a combination of big ambition, grateful condition, and savage persistence, he has helped hundreds of clients optimize their family income, accelerate their family bank velocity, and create lasting legacies.

A passionate advocate for integrating faith with business success, Wesley serves as a volunteer speaker and teacher. His approach to entrepreneurship emphasizes that contentment and ambition are not opposing forces, but rather complementary elements essential for living a rich life full of enjoyment, satisfaction, and meaning.

Wesley is the author of *From Busy to Rich* and *What Do You Do?* He and his wife, Jamie, as well as their two children, Gage and Abby, live in Austin, Texas.